THE ENGLISH BO.
(1872
and
RECORD BOOK

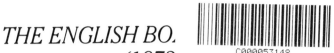

Bill Matthews

ARTHUR H. STOCKWELL LTD.
Elms Court   Ilfracombe
Devon

Cover illustration — Samuel Blakelock

ISBN 0 7223 2413-8

Printed in Great Britain by
Arthur H. Stockwell Ltd.
Elms Court   Ilfracombe
Devon

INDEX

Illustrations set at rear of book.

List of Illustrations:

BOXERS' RECORD SECTION

THE ENGLISH BOXING CHAMPIONS
(1872-1910)

PREFACE

After the near demise of the Prize Ring in 1867, brought about by new legislation making it a criminal offence to convey sportsmen to a prize-fight, boxing still continued as it had done for years in the numerous sparring saloons that existed throughout the country. There the professional boxer could earn money by participating in gloved bouts. These were classed as exhibitions and as such were allowed by law. Every boxing saloon had its own regular performers and champions.

In 1868 the Marquis of Queensbury put his name to a new set of rules governing contests with gloves, and this assisted in making the sport more acceptable to the general public.

Competition boxing soon became popular, and in 1872 the famous Bow Cups were inaugurated in order to discover who the champions were in this style of boxing.

Some of the professional boxers were not happy about the rule limiting contests to four rounds only, and by 1877 the first of the 'duration' title bouts took place.

Championship Competitions continued to be held for many years, but by the 1890s the recognized champions of the time seldom took part in them. Consequently some of the winners of these competitions were of a very poor class indeed, and would have stood no chance against the official champion. Nevertheless they are a part of boxing history and as such should be recorded.

This book is the result of many years of research and contains details relating to champions whose deeds hitherto have gone unrecorded. Among them surprisingly are a number of World Champions. I have made a particular study of the Middleweight Division, and the results of my research completely alter the concept of the early history of this class.

CHAPTER ONE

TOM ALLEN

Tom Allen was born in the City of Birmingham in 1839 of humble parents, who because of their poverty were unable to have their son properly educated. So from an early age young Tom had to earn his living. He became by trade a gunmaker, and in his spare time he accompanied his brother Harry to the various sparring saloons of the neighbourhood. In this way they were able not only to pick up a good knowledge of the game, but also to earn for themselves a few extra coppers.

Allen's first recorded ring contest was with Morris Connor, whom he defeated in forty-two minutes for a £20 stake; this was in March 1861.

In November of the same year he was matched against Jack Gould at 9st. 10lb. Again he gained the victory after fighting for sixty-five minutes.

His first set-back was when he was defeated by the Waggoner in thirty minutes.

Tom then went on to defeat White, a fellow townsman for a stake of £10; but in his next outing was beaten by that formidable Midlander, Posh Price in fifty minutes.

He rested for eighteen months before being matched against Bingley Rose of Nottingham, for £50 a-side, at 10st. For this contest Allen got himself into the best possible condition, but his unfortunate opponent had an attack of boils which completely covered his body. He had no right to be in the ring in such condition, but the alternative was to forfeit the stakes.

Despite his poor condition his impetuous fighting over the first four rounds gave him a decided edge. Tom, however, remained calm and when Rose slowed down, he began to hit his opponent all over the ring, Bingley being compelled to give in after fighting for twenty-two minutes.

Allen's backers now went for bigger game and matched their man

9

against the unbeaten coloured pugilist Bob Smith of America, who was about the best welterweight in the country at that time.

In this contest Smith was always in the ascendancy, and beat his game opponent in a contest lasting two hours and fifteen minutes.

Tom rested for another year during which time his weight increased by almost a stone. It was at 10st. 12lb. that he was matched against Jack Parkinson, also of Birmingham, for £25 a-side.

Allen was not in the best condition for this fight, but gained an early advantage when he floored his man with a heavy right-hander. Tom pressed home his advantage but was too impetuous, and missed with several heavy punches. Parkinson made the mistake of closing with his opponent, and was grasped firmly, and hurled down upon the hard ground.

Jack, however, was not yet beaten and he lured Allen into a corner, and there waited until Tom let go with a swinging punch. Parkinson ducked swiftly beneath the blow, and Allen's fist smashed into the corner post, knocking up his hand for the remainder of the contest. Jack tried to take advantage of the situation, but in trying to throw his adversary, he was himself thrown, cracking his head on the ground.

He never recovered from this and Tom proceeded to punish him severely; one punch in particular cutting Jack's cheek to the bone. He was a badly beaten fighter when the police authorities came on the scene, causing the fight to be abandoned.

The men were ordered to renew hostilities at a later date, but Parkinson failed to appear, victory going to Allen by default.

Tom's next contest was a return bout against Posh Price, who was no longer the fighter of old. Nevertheless it took Allen over two hours to subdue the veteran.

George Iles of Bristol was Tom's next opponent. The Bristol man having all the physical advantages, being 4in. the taller man, and 19lb. the heavier.

In the earlier rounds Allen had great difficulty in reaching his opponent, and when he did venture in close, he was invariably thrown. Fortunately for the Brum his opponent had been over-trained, and he soon began to show signs of weakness. Tom now started to get home with his heavier punches, and poor George was dazed by the sudden change. Iles could not understand his apparent weakness, and as the fight went on he tired perceptively, enabling Allen to punish him unmercifully. George was game to the core and kept coming up for round after round, in a cause that was completely hopeless. Even the ring-hardened veterans were sickened by the punishment he was taking.

Belatedly after fighting for sixty-two minutes, Bob Brettle threw up the sponge in token of defeat.

Allen was fortunate in securing such an easy victory, but his reputation as a pugilist was made.

Now came Tom's most important match to date, his opponent being Joe Goss of Wolverhampton. The date for the contest was March 5th, 1867, and it was one of the last important fights of the old Prize Ring in this country.

Once again good fortune favoured Allen, for Goss had only come out of prison fourteen days prior to the contest, he having been present at the Peter Morris — George Holden fight, for which he had received a month's imprisonment. Tom in contrast was trained to perfection. When they went to scale Joe tipped the beam at 11st. 10lb., an advantage of 7lb. over the Brum.

For one hour and forty-two minutes they hammered away at each other, the lead alternating first with one, then the other. They fought in grand style, until in the end they had both literally punched themselves out. Both sides then conferred together, and a draw was mutually agreed upon.

In July of 1867, Allen in company with Peter Morris and Bill Ryall, decided to try their luck in America. It was not, however, until January 1869 that he met the veteran Bill Davis for $1000 a-side, with the American Heavyweight Title at stake.

Davis started off extremely well, knocking Allen down cleanly to end the first round. In the following round he also drew first blood, thus winning the first two events. Tom then pulled himself together and began to show his true form, and proceeded to administer a beating to his American foe. Only the gameness of the veteran enabled him to last until the 43rd round, when Tom succeeded in knocking him out, thus securing his first victory on American soil.

There were other claimants to the American title, among them being Charlie Gallagher of Canada. The latter was not considered to be in the same class as the Briton, but created a great surprise by landing a crashing punch to Allen's jugular vein. Not only did it knock poor Tom out, it very nearly killed him! The whole fight lasted just three minutes!

The Brum soon recovered from this shock defeat and matched himself against another claimant to the title, Mike McCoole of Ireland.

From the start Allen outclassed his foe, punishing his man severely. This was too much for Mike's supporters to endure, and they invaded the ring and threatened the referee at gunpoint to declare their man the winner of the fight on a foul. This the sensible man did, thus escaping with his life!

Two months later Tom had a return fight with Charlie Gallagher, and was easily beating his man when again his opponent's supporters prevented the fight from continuing, after they had been in the ring for twenty-five minutes.

Allen now became an American citizen, realising that this was the only way he was going to get fair play whilst he was in that country.

It was about this time that Jem Mace arrived in America, and a fight was quickly ratified between the two for the World Heavyweight Championship.

Needless to say Tom was completely outclassed by the master boxer, after a contest lasting forty-four minutes. He did, however, have the satisfaction of knocking Mace clean off his legs during the bout.

In October of 1870, Allen met Charlie Gallagher for the third time, and on this occasion proceeded to thrash his man in only twenty-three and a half minutes.

Jem Mace announced his retirement in 1872, which left the World Heavyweight title vacant. Tom was matched against Mike McCoole for only $250 a-side, with the premier title at stake.

On this occasion Allen made short work of his opponent, winning easily in only twenty minutes.

Ben Hogan of Germany challenged for the title, and they met on November 18th, 1873.

In the 3rd round a dispute arose, which quickly turned into a full scaled riot. Tom had, however, proved himself to be the better man, and the stakes were awarded to him.

Joe Goss, Allen's old rival was now in America in company with Jem Mace, and both men were prepared to fight Tom for the title. Wisely Allen made a match with Goss, but before he met Joe in defence of his title, he fought Mace with the gloves, and as expected he was beaten on points by the old master.

Goss had not fought since his last battle with Allen some nine years earlier, and it was thought that he would be stale after so long an absence from the ring.

From the start, however, Joe was the aggressor, although after a few rounds had been fought he was blowing hard. Allen succeeded in closing one of Joe's eyes, and it did look as though Tom would eventually win. But the fight was given to Goss on an alleged foul, Allen striking his opponent when the latter was on the ground. Tom bitterly disputed the decision, and he decided to return to England.

He quickly made it known that he was prepared to challenge the world, and waited for a response. It was thought that the English champion John Knifton would accept, but although the latter was willing enough, his backers were more prudent, and the proposed match fell through.

It was left to a complete novice in Tomkin Gilbert of Lincoln to accept the challenge, and fight for what was advertised as the World Heavyweight Championship, the first under Marquis of Queensbury Rules.

Allen thought little of his opponent for he entered the ring as fat as an ox. Gilbert too looked as though his training had been neglected.

Tomkin led off with his left, but in attempting to repeat the blow was countered heavily on the cheek. This riled the Lincoln man who rushed in wildly, but he was met with a stinging punch that landed on his nose, drawing the blood. The infuriated Gilbert again stormed in, but was countered by Tom's right. Allen then stepped back and sent a swinging left-hander that landed on his opponent's forehead, dropping him to his knees.

Tomkin attempted to lead off but was countered yet again with a smashing punch to the nose, drawing the blood in streams. They closed, Tom fighting at the head, Gilbert to the body. After the rally they broke away, completely winded by their exertions. Tom seeing the condition of his opponent, crashed home a punch to the mouth that sent the novice to the floor again.

Allen forced the fighting, and the luckless Gilbert, whose nose was in an awful mess, looked completely dazed by the punishment he had received. He still, however, gamely rushed at his foe with the intention of punching his man about the ribs. The Brum stepped back and crashed home an uppercut that caused Gilbert to reel around the ring. Recovering he lunged at Allen, but fell in the attempt.

The seconds of the Lincoln man advised their man to force the pace. He attempted to do so and a rally ensued, in which no damage was sustained by either man. Again Tom got home with an uppercut, and Gilbert lay stretched out on the floor.

Tomkin now boxed with caution or trepidation, and this suited Allen who was in need of a breather. Consequently in a rather scrambling round, no damage was done.

Allen went up to his man, feinted with the left, drawing Gilbert's guard down, then crashed home a right-hander to the jaw. Tomkin made a weak effort to fight back and punish Tom about the body. In doing so he sent in a blow below the belt that warranted disqualification. Allen backed away and sent left after left to Gilbert's sore nose, and the latter ended the round by falling to his knees.

The Brum went on to the attack and shot home left and right to Tomkin's head; they closed and once again the Lincoln man hit low. This riled Tom who caught his opponent by the arms, and twisted him over with the assistance of a back heel! An appeal for a foul was made but the referee ordered the two men to fight on. Gilbert, however, had had enough, and despite the entreaties of his seconds, he refused to fight any more. So Allen won the 'World Heavyweight Championship' in a contest that lasted sixteen minutes and twenty-five seconds.

Allen looked round for fresh challengers. John Knifton had now gone to relations in America, and there did not seem to be anyone capable of extending him.

It came as a surprise when the former middleweight champion challenged Tom for the championship. Charley Davis had retired some years before due to a serious illness. At his best he would have been quite a formidable challenger, but his illness had robbed him of his physical powers.

Allen on this occasion scaled 13st. 7lb., but it was obvious that he had made no serious attempt to get himself into shape. Considering his age, however, he didn't appear to be in too bad a condition.

His opponent Davis was no longer the boxer of former times. The grand muscular development of his chest, back, and shoulders were no more. The illness that had caused his retirement had left him but a shadow of the man he had once been.

To begin with there was a good deal of sparring, before Davis led out with his left. Allen jumped nimbly away, but coming again he received a light punch to the mark, to which he replied with a left-hander to the jaw. Towards the end of the round the crowd began to get impatient with the rather tedious sparring. Roused by the jeers and catcalls of the spectators, the two men indulged in a short but furious rally, Charley being forced down. On rising, Tom was in no hurry to follow up his advantage, and they sparred until time was called.

Davis was urged to go for Allen's rather corpulent body; this remark was heard by Tom who took up the offensive. Toe to toe they slammed away at each other until Davis was sent reeling from a left-hander to the jaw. Fortunately for Charley a cry of "Police!" was heard, but it proved to be a false alarm. The time lost in the confusion, however, allowed Davis to recover. He was still weak and Allen had all the best of the exchanges. Charley did land a couple of punches when Tom missed with a vicious upper-cut. The Brum took the initiative and handed out severe punishment to his now beaten opponent.

Gamely Davis answered the call of "Time!" and Allen proceeded to knock him all over the ring until he was forced down. He arose just in time but was immediately sent down again. Painfully he forced himself upright, only to take two more punches that sent him senseless to the floor. His second, Jack Hicks, entered the ring to pick up his man, deliberately getting Davis disqualified. The five round contest had lasted eighteen minutes and twenty-five seconds.

Tom was allowed to rest on his laurels for a year before the Scotsman Jem Stewart signed to meet him for the title. Allen was now thirty-eight years old, and his opponent thirty-five.

For the first time since his return to this country, Tom got himself into a first-class condition. At the weigh in he scaled 13st. 2lb. to Jem's 12st. 2lb.

As a championship battle it was a great disappointment. Stewart showed great respect (or fear) for the champion, and rarely made any attempt to fight. Consequently the bout developed into a tedious sparring match, that roused the unfortunate spectators to hiss and boo throughout.

After a farcical contest lasting one hour and forty minutes, the referee, to the relief of the bored onlookers, stopped the fight and declared it a draw. Why Tom did not go after his mediocre opponent remains a mystery. Had he done so he would easily have beaten the Scotsman, who was not in the same class as a boxer.

Unfortunately the bout did nothing to popularise the sport of glove fighting, and boxing went into a decline for a number of years.

Allen never defended the title again. When John L. Sullivan came to the fore in 1882, Tom returned to America with the intention of fighting the new sensation.

In November of 1882, he boxed an exhibition with George Rooke, and the form he displayed on this occasion was so pathetic, that it was obvious his fighting days were over. He did, however, enter the ring on one other occasion to fight an exhibition with Fiddler Neary; this was in January 1884, and it terminated a career that had lasted for thirty-three years.

On his retirement Allen became a saloon keeper in the City of New Orleans, and became quite successful and prosperous in that enterprise.

He died in that city on April 5th, 1904, aged sixty-four.

CHAPTER TWO

BILL BAXTER

Bill Baxter was born on October 16th, 1860, and was the eldest of four
brothers, all of whom featured in the ring during the 1880s and 1890s.
He learned his boxing in a hard but efficient school. Boxing was
permitted on licensed premises then, and attached to them were the
sparring rooms, usually managed by an old pugilist. It was in the
Shoreditch area of London that young William was instructed in the art
of self-defence. The 'Blue Anchor' in Church Street presided over by Bill
Richardson, and later by Tom Symonds, was one of those houses
frequented by Baxter. Corrections of stance, head, and footwork, were
strictly insisted upon; in fact a lad was taught the science of boxing from
A to Z.

Having had to fight a number of endurance battles, he early
recognized that moving unnecessarily around the ring was a waste of
energy. He would invariably take up a position as near to the centre of
the ring as possible, there he would pivot around, and allow his
opponent to do all the running. It was as an exponent of the straight left
that Baxter earned just fame. Few boxers of his day could equal the
precision of hitting that he achieved, and over a lengthy journey he was
unbeatable at his weight.

With his cool methodical style he required time to formulate and
carry out a plan of campaign. Although he finished as a finalist in many
competitions that he entered, where the opposition was at its strongest,
he was not successful in carrying off the prizes.

He did win Bob Habbijam's 8st. 6lb. Champion's Belt Competition,
and in 1886 he defeated Pudsey Sullivan on points over twelve rounds,
to win Harry Clark's Champion's Belt. He also won three competitions
at nine stone, on one occasion defeating his brother Sam in the final
over four rounds.

He met Fred Johnson of Hackney on about a dozen occasions, the
latter invariably winning over the shorter route in competitions. But on

16

December 21st, 1888, he met Johnson in a duration bout for the Bantamweight (8st. 6lb.) Title. The fight took place at the Kennington Social Club, in a small, low-ceilinged, and ill-ventilated room. The fight was announced as "Twenty rounds or more", which in effect meant a fight to the finish.

Baxter started off in his usual methodical way, which allowed Johnson with his fast hands to build up an early lead. The skill shown by both men was superb. Baxter would keep in the centre of the ring, wheeling around in a small circle, shifting his head sideways as the blows of Johnson rattled about him. A movement of an inch was all that he required to escape a swing, while his right parried many a well-intentioned straight left.

Bill was always looking for an opening for his left hand, and when he did have the opportunity, he shot it out with the full weight of his body behind it, sometimes following it up with a right to the ribs.

After ten rounds had been got through Johnson was still a shade in front, but it was noticeable that Bill's left-handers were taking effect, and he slowly but surely began to forge ahead. The Hackney man fought back fiercely and landed many a hard blow, but the longer the battle went on, the further Baxter went ahead.

In the 42nd round Johnson could fight no more, and Bill was declared the winner and champion, after a fight that had lasted two hours and forty-seven minutes.

Having established himself as champion, Bill was besieged by challenges to fight over the shorter distance, but none would meet him in a duration fight. He was kept extremely busy, however, and continued to enter competition boxing.

In February 1889 he was outpointed by Fred Johnson over four rounds, for the title of 8st. 8lb. Champion. In the following March he entered a 9st. Championship Competition, and in the final met Harry Mead. It was a good bout and Baxter was in top form. He was conceding quite a bit of weight, but he thoroughly outpointed his man. It was a bitter blow to him when the decision was given to Mead! In the same month he came up against Fred Johnson again in the final of an 8st. 12lb. competition, and once more the decision was given against him. It was in the April of 1889 that he defeated his brother Sam over four rounds, to win a 9st. Championship Competition.

In January 1890 Morgan Crowther challenged Baxter to a duration contest for £100 a-side. Although not mentioned in the report it is probable that Bill's Bantamweight Title was on the line. The fight was to a finish with 2oz. gloves being used. The venue was Barney Sheppard's place in Mountford Street, Kennington.

After a cautious start the men got to work. The Welshman suddenly dashed in and landed a terrific punch with his left to Bill's kidneys.

B

Baxter was badly hurt but contrived to keep the true state of affairs from his opponent. He was almost paralysed down the right side as a result of the blow, and had the greatest difficulty in standing upright. But the half-humorous, half-grim expression never left his face, and keeping to the centre of the ring, he made Crowther do all the running. It was with a sense of relief that the round came to an end. There were anxious enquiries from his seconds who knew something was wrong. "I can't use my right hand, but don't worry, I'll be alright soon" Bill said. But it was not until the 8th round that Baxter recovered from that cruel blow. It was in this round that Bill started to fight back for the first time. With wonderful precision and severity he banged his left to his opponent's nose and mouth, until Crowther was fairly staggered by the rapidity of the Londoner's attack. The Welshman tried desperately to evade the shower of punches that rained on him from all directions, and his nose and mouth soon resembled a piece of raw liver.

Game and strong though he was Crowther soon became winded; his nostrils were becoming clogged up, and his lips were so swollen and cut, that it was with the greatest difficulty that he could breathe. Baxter took full advantage of his foe's discomfiture, and rained a fusilade of punches on his half-choked opponent. The courageous Welshman withstood the onslaught till the 17th round, by which time he was forced to surrender.

At this time Baxter was at his peak. He became involved with the eccentric sportsman Squire Abingdon, who offered to back him for £1,000 against anyone in the world. Specific challenges were made to George Dixon and Ike Weir, but they chose to ignore them. After waiting for three months the generous sportsman withdrew the money, and paid it over to Bill.

Soon afterwards the Pelican Club arranged a twenty round match between Bill and his old rival Fred Johnson.

As usual Baxter allowed his opponent to do the running, and contented himself with occasionally popping over his left into his opponent's face. Fred not relishing these punches, attempted to keep the fight at close quarters, where he believed his rapid two-handed hitting would give him the advantage.

Half-way through round six whilst they were engaged in close quarter work, Johnson threw a punch to the body which unfortunately went well below the belt, causing Baxter to sink to the floor. The referee had no option but to give the decision to the Shoreditch man.

The blow was of course accidental, and the club members were anxious to see the pair perform again. So only a week later the two old rivals faced each other once more.

The contest was fought in the most sportsmanlike manner, with both boxers displaying scrupulous fairness. In fact Baxter missed many opportunities of winning by standing back when he had his opponent in difficulties. Twice he had Johnson at his mercy, but instead of going in and finishing his man, he walked away and allowed Fred to recover. At the finish the two judges disagreed, and the referee gave his casting vote to Johnson.

Baxter now had a lengthy rest before entering a £100 competition held at the Kennington Social Club. He fought his way to the final, and there he had to meet Ginger Elmer of Notting Hill. As usual he was giving away a considerable amount of weight to his opponent, but his superior boxing appeared to give him the edge, but to the surprise of the onlookers, Elmer was given the decision.

Now in his thirty-first year Baxter decided to become a boxing instructor, and opened up a school at Hanley, where he was quite successful.

The National Sporting Club were looking for an opponent for Billy Reader of Hatcham, to fight for the 9st. Title, and the fight was offered to Baxter. He had to concede about 7lb. to his opponent, although he was 2½in. the taller man. He got himself into the best possible shape, but after ten years in the ring, the elasticity of youth was absent.

For the first ten rounds it was the old Baxter. His timing and judgement were superb, and the accuracy of his hitting made a sorry mess of Reader. But the latter was game to the core, and no amount of punishment seemed to stop him.

After the tenth round it was noticeable that the veteran was tiring, and Reader, still doggedly moving forward, drove both hands to Baxter's body with considerable force. The Shoreditch man could not conceal that he was hurt; his left was still accurate, but it now lacked power.

In the 16th round Reader landed a tremendous punch to Baxter's midsection, and for the first time in his career the veteran had the fatal ten counted over him.

Bill returned to Hanley, but not wishing to retire on a losing note, issued a challenge to box anyone at his weight, i.e. 8st. 8lb. Had he kept to this things would have been alright, but Stanton Abbott was keen to meet Baxter, but only at 9st. Eventually Bill agreed to this but found the grind of training a drudgery. He looked well enough on the night, but he was now undoubtedly stale.

The fight was a great disappointment. Baxter fought the worst fight of his life. He just could not get the timing of his punches and in consequence suffered a humiliating defeat, being defeated by a knockout in the 12th round.

Baxter had three more bouts that brought his career to an end. Against his old foe Fred Johnson he was defeated on points over six rounds. He was then successful in beating Charlie Williams, and in his final bout he outpointed Harry Mead over six rounds, at the N.S.C.

He was invited by that organisation to act as one of the resident seconds of the club, and for a number of years he fulfilled those duties.

CHAPTER THREE

SAMUEL BLAKELOCK

Samuel Blakelock was born in Battersea, London, on June 10th, 1864. His father was a chimney-sweep by trade and young Sam initially followed that calling.

Despite family opposition he became interested in the sport of boxing, and frequented many of the sparring saloons situated south of the river. In the early days he often bore marks of punishment he had received, and his mother would give him a 'tongue lashing' over his 'evil ways'. Her opposition disappeared, however, when he began to bring home the golden sovereigns, the results of the numerous competitions he had won.

Sam commenced boxing in 1880 and won thirty consecutive competitions, one of them being a 9st. Championship held at Long Acres in the West End. In the final of which he defeated Tom Stirk.

Tom Euston challenged him to a fight with the knuckles, and this took place in the year 1888; Blakelock winning very easily in only seven minutes. So convincing was his victory over Euston, that no one ever challenged him to fight with nature's weapons again.

Sam went to America but failed to get a match on. It was during this trip that he met John L. Sullivan, the American champion, and the pair became good friends. Not being able to get anyone to meet him, however, he decided to return home.

His first opponent on his return was Tom Euston, this time using the gloves. The result was another easy victory for the Battersea man.

John L. Sullivan now came to this country and Sam was established as a member of his team. He was in John's corner in France when the latter fought Charlie Mitchell for the World Heavyweight Title.

After Sullivan returned to America, Blakelock found things very quiet in this country, and once more sailed over to America. After a considerable amount of haggling he was matched with fellow countryman Jimmy Carroll, for one version of the World Lightweight

Title. The contest was held at the famous Californian Athletic Club in San Francisco. For the first time in his career Sam was beaten, being knocked out in the 16th round.

Returning home, he was matched with the up and coming Fulham boxer Billy Reader, the contest taking place at Ashley's Amphitheatre in Westminster Bridge Road.

Sam was supremely confident at the start of the fight, for Billy was one of those in and out boxers. Unfortunately for Blakelock he caught Reader on one of his best days. He attempted to keep the fight at long range, but despite hitting his adversary with considerable force, he was unable to keep him at bay. The Fulham man ignored Sam's left-handers and bored in to close quarters. Reader was a brilliant in-fighter, and sticking close to Sam, he dealt out severe punishment. Blakelock fought back resolutely and tried to knock his opponent out, but he never had the power of punch to achieve this. After fighting the full twelve rounds Reader was awarded the decision.

For a while after this Sam did not enjoy the best of health, and it took some time before he could get himself back into fighting condition.

In the spring of 1890, he was matched against Dave Burke at the Kennington Social Club. Burke on his day was a brilliant performer, who had beaten some of the best men of the period, and he was greatly fancied to defeat the Battersea man.

It was a good contest while it lasted, but from the start Blakelock took a decided lead. The contest terminated suddenly, however, when Burke was disqualified for striking a low blow.

Jem Verrall of Peckham was Sam's next opponent, and the contest took place at the Ormonde Club in the Walworth Road.

It was one of the most bloody and bitter bouts ever seen; and after a savage fight lasting seventeen rounds, Sam was carried from the ring a beaten man. This fight practically finished the careers of both men, for Verrall never fought again, and Sam fought only once more.

His last opponent was Reuben Baxter and Sam finished his career on a victorious note by defeating his man over fifteen rounds.

After his retirement from the ring Blakelock was in great demand as a trainer and second, but the sport of horse-racing now held a greater attraction for him. For a time he became a bookmaker, but unfortunately he was one of the few who did not become prosperous at it.

He promoted several boxing shows that were of a high standard, but his interest in the sport appeared to wane, for after 1904 he was rarely seen in boxing circles.

CHAPTER FOUR

CHARLEY DAVIS

Michael Davis who was later better known as Charley Davis, was born in Stepney, London in 1849.

As a young man he was employed as a van driver, first as a carrier of ginger beer, and later plate glass. He lost both jobs because his employers objected to his connection with the sport of boxing. He was a regular performer at Bill Richardson's establishment, the 'Blue Anchor', situated in Shoreditch. When he lost his second job he was offered the position of head waiter and bouncer at the 'Blue Anchor' — a position he accepted gladly.

In those early days he was a perfect physical specimen, with fine shoulders, powerful neck, long and strong arms, and good thighs and legs; a powerful-looking man. He was not tall, being only 5ft. 7in. in height. His face had a Jewish look about it, but was fresh and healthy-looking.

He first came into prominence in February 1872, when in a boxing competition for a silver cup valued at £20, he first defeated Abe Daultrey, and later in the final met the famous pugilist Bat Mullins.

Mullins was the cleverer boxer of the two, and early in the contest he undoubtedly had the edge, but the concession of about 1½st. in weight began to tell, and eventually Charley's strong attacks wore the little man down; Davis receiving the decision.

Eight days later he competed again for a silver cup. In the first round he disposed of Obadiah Atterbury; but in the final was defeated by the ex-featherweight champion Jack Hicks.

Shortly afterwards he seconded Tom Callas when the latter fought Jack Connor. Unfortunately Callas died and Davis was arrested. On the night of his arrest (May 13th) he defeated Denny Harrington in a competition in which a silver cup had been donated. The police officers were sporting enough to wait until the boxing was completed before taking Charley into custody. In the following July all parties concerned

23

in the fatal fight were tried at the Maidstone Assizes and acquitted.

The Bow Championship cups were now attracting attention. The first holder of the Middleweight Title Trophy was Bill Brooks, but the unfortunate man died whilst in training. This left the title vacant and Davis was matched against John McConnell in a duration bout, which meant that it was a battle to the finish, the first championship fight of its kind with gloves.

McConnell was Irish born although he had lived in Glasgow since infancy. His first contest had been with Boyle, with whom he had drawn. He then went on to defeat Bill Poole and Jem Stewart. His only defeat had come in a competition, when he had been beaten by D. Young.

Finding it impossible to get any more matches north of the border, he decided to try his luck in England. It is said that he walked all the way down to London. Once there he made his way to Nat Langham's establishment, where a trial was quickly arranged for the new-comer. Plantagenet Green, a tricky fighter was opposed to him, but it took McConnell only two rounds to knock out his coloured adversary. Present on this occasion was Joe Goss who was instrumental in collecting a purse for the winner.

McConnell now moved over to Bill Richardson's place, and after several bouts there soon became a favourite. It was Bill Richardson who backed the Irishman for £50 against his former star boxer.

The venue for the bout was Albert Austin's gymnasium in Blomfield Street. It was a somewhat ramshackle place and unsafe as it proved before the fight commenced, for a staircase collapsed! — but fortunately nobody was injured by the falling masonry.

There was a further delay when it was discovered that the bag in which McConnell kept his ring gear was missing, and it took some time before substitute garments could be found. When McConnell entered the ring there was much laughter when the crowd saw how he was dressed. The old pair of cricketing trousers that he wore had been made for a man at least a foot shorter, and considerably wider! They were creased and dirty with two black patches in the seat of the pants!

Davis was well supplied with corner necessities, including ice, etc., but poor 'Scotty' had nothing. But at Charley's suggestion some of the ice was handed over to his opponent's corner. Bill Kennard was nominated as the referee, and he read the articles to the men before the bout started. These stipulated that the rounds were of 3-minute duration, with a minute's rest between each round. Shortly afterwards they shook hands and commenced the battle.

McConnell stood well over his man, being some 2½in. the taller. He looked strong and was obviously in excellent condition. Davis appeared to have a bit of a 'tummy', but this was usual for him. He looked strong and was as awkward looking as ever, holding his head well back out of danger, whilst extending his left arm. He was cautious to begin with, allowing the Irishman to manoeuvre round the ring. At length they came together, McConnell lashing out with a right-hander, but missed as Davis jumped back. Charley now came in and scored with a heavy right-hander, that knocked his opponent down. Scotty got up immediately but received another right-hander on the ear. Instead of following up his advantage Davis boxed cautiously and tried to keep the fight at long range, but McConnell continually bustled into him, but no more effective blows were landed by either man.

Soon after the start of the 3rd round, McConnell sent Davis to the boards with a heavy right-hander. Charley at this stage looked none too comfortable, for the Irishman continued to force the pace and definitely had the better of the exchanges. Davis in attempting to get away was grasped by McConnell, who was about to throw him down when cries of "Foul!" induced the Irishman to let him go. For this infringement he was cautioned by the referee, who ordered the fight to be continued. Almost immediately afterwards McConnell was floored by a right-hander to the ear.

The next three rounds were in favour of Scotty, who fought in great style; Davis at times appearing to be in difficulties. The latter, however, fought back resolutely and had the satisfaction of twice flooring his opponent, although he was still getting the worst of the exchanges. Both were winded by their exertions, but the Irishman still maintained his lead.

A change came in the 12th round when Davis appeared to be the stronger of the two, for he shook McConnell on several occasions with his heavy punches.

McConnell weakened and he was unable to keep his eager foe at bay with his left hand. Davis followed up his advantage and used both hands with great effect, until the Irishman went down in his own corner; Charley looming over his man, ready to knock him down as soon as he arose. Gamely McConnell faced his opponent but was immediately floored again. He had barely struggled to his feet when he was again knocked down by a heavy punch. This proved to be the finisher and the sponge was thrown up by his corner; Davis winning a gruelling battle.

Because of the way the fight terminated, a new rule was introduced allowing a man who was floored ten seconds in which to regain his feet. If he failed to do so he would be 'Knocked out of time'.

Charley was now surprisingly challenged by Ted Napper, the former 8st. 10lb. bare knuckle champion, at which weight he had remained unbeaten. His many challenges to the world had gone unanswered. He was now, however, thirty-two years of age and considered to be too stale to contend with such a man as Davis.

No time was lost in making the arrangements, and the men were matched for the Middleweight Title, the fight to take place in the following April.

Grafton Hall in Soho, a former chapel, was the venue for the fight, and on the night in question about 250 boxing fans paid their sovereign entrance fee. Jack Vandy was appointed as referee and he viewed the contest from the former pulpit!

Napper had to concede 7lb. in weight to his adversary, as well as eight years in age. It was obvious that he was but a shadow of his former self, but he seemed confident enough as he faced his opponent.

Davis was in no hurry to start; he stood with his head thrown well back, his left arm well extended, waiting for the older man to take the initiative. This Ted proceeded to do, landing several left-handers and cleverly avoiding the returns by a graceful and rapid skip to the rear, that was particularly his own. Charley was unworried by the frequent visitations, relying on countering his opponent, which he succeeded in doing, landing the occasional heavy punch.

The earlier rounds were definitely in favour of the veteran, but as the fight progressed Napper started to weaken.

In the 23rd round Ted hit Charley with a heavy blow to the face that drove him across the ring, and following it up rapidly, he let go a right-hander that deposited Davis on the floor! The champion was up in an instant and vigorously went after his man, forcing a rally and generally getting the better of it.

They both came out fighting in the next round and banged away at each other; Napper in attempting a punch, fell sprawling to the floor.

When Charley tried to finish off his opponent in the next round, he found it extremely difficult for Ted was surrounded by his seconds, preventing him from getting in a clean hit. After rather a scrambling three minutes the round ended.

Napper was now a beaten man and he conceded defeat, after a contest lasting one hour and twenty-four minutes.

Davis now went on a sparring tour with Denny Harrington and the two became great friends. When Charley announced his retirement in June 1876 because of ill-health, it was Harrington that claimed his old friend's title.

Davis like so many champions before him (and since!) lived the high life, and like many of them he paid the price. He contracted a nasty illness which left him with a diseased kidney, and his fighting days were considered to be over. Five years later, however, he stupidly consented to meet Tom Allen for the latter's heavyweight title, in which he was easily defeated.

He was obviously still a very sick man for it was only two years later that he died at the tragically early age of thirty.

CHAPTER FIVE

GEORGE DOVE

Dove came from the East End of London, that hot-bed of pugilism from which so many good champions sprang. From an early age George showed a natural aptitude for the sport, being by nature an aggressive individual. In the 1860s, he was one of the many youngsters who used to tour the West End sparring saloons, earning themselves a little money by frequent exhibitions with the gloves. These were not the mild affairs of the present day, but real fights, featuring some of the finest boxing ever seen among the bantam boxers.

Dove was a regular visitor to Bill Richardson's place situated in Shoreditch and soon impressed the experts there with his proficiency with the gloves.

At this time the Prize Ring was in its death throes and it was some time before George was matched for a small sum against William Lead. Lead's reputation with the gloves was even greater than that of Dove, so an interesting scrap was anticipated.

George was about 5ft. 3in. in height and scaled on this occasion about 7st. 4lb. His round face, highlighted by his piercing eyes, bore a determined look.

The 1st round lasted some twenty minutes, during which George did more or less what he liked with his opponent, although Lead tried all he knew to thwart his foe. It eventually dawned on Bill that he was up against a better man, and proceeded to fight on in the hope that the police would show up and stop the fight.

After fighting for an hour, Dove had built up a clear lead, and looked a certainty to win. Then unfortunately for him the police did put in an appearance, and efforts were made to find another venue. But before a site could be located an agreement was made whereupon George would receive £4 if he would agree to a draw. So ended Dove's first entry into the prize ring.

Efforts were made to get a match on with Perkins of Mile End, but twice the latter forfeited. George remained inactive until 1866, when a new Jewish pugilist came to the fore. This was Wolf Cohen and his people of the East End were ecstatic about their new champion. The men were matched for £15 a-side.

Cohen had all the physical advantages over his opponent. He was the taller man, longer in reach, and a good 14lb. the heavier.

After a few feints and passes they settled down to real work. Cohen landed his left to the body but was countered smartly on the right temple by George's left, this being followed by a right-hander to the body. Cohen retaliated with a light left to Dove's left eye. Being the shorter man, George kept feinting at Cohen's face, with the intention of drawing his opponent's guard up, so that he could hit him about the body. Eventually the Jew did raise his guard by a couple of inches, and like lightning George drove in a right-hander to the mark. In attempting to repeat the blow, however, he was short. Both now countered, Wolf getting home on the throat, and George on the right cheek. Dove succeeded in landing a terrific right to the body, then Wolf countering with a right to the ribs. After fighting for only 3½ minutes the police showed up, and a new venue was sought.

In the new ring George quickly took the lead. His punching was the heavier of the two and soon Cohen began to fight shy. Steadily Dove increased his lead although Cohen now fought back in resolute fashion. When the Jew's left hand went things began to look bad for him. Several times he appeared to be on the brink of defeat, but fought back with great courage, but after fighting for two hours he was compelled to give in.

This completed Dove's bare knuckle career and he probably went back to the sparring saloons.

In 1872 competitions with the gloves started to become popular and George entered one of these in January of that year, but was defeated by Alec Lawson in two rounds. In the following month he succeeded in winning an 8st. 4lb. competition, defeating J. Hickton over three rounds.

When the famous Bow Cups were inaugurated at five different weights to find out who the champions were, George entered the Bantamweight class at 8st. 4lb. In the first round he defeated George Cunningham; then in the semifinal he gained his revenge over Alec Lawson. The final was over five rounds and he was opposed to Jerry Hawkes, whom he defeated on points.

Hawkes was dissatisfied with this defeat and repeatedly over the years challenged his conqueror to another battle. This challenge was eventually accepted and they agreed to meet in August 1877 with the English Bantamweight Title at stake.

This bout proved to be a fiasco for in the first minute of the second round George connected with a right-hander to Hawke's neck, and Jerry crumpled to the floor. Although he could have risen Hawke decided that discretion was better than valour, and stayed down until counted out!

Later in the same evening George agreed to fight an exhibition with Bob Habbijam. This proved to be an exciting scrap that delighted the onlookers after the disappointment of the titular affair.

After his retirement from the ring Dove started a new career as a coin manipulator, and could be seen at fairs and racecourses performing the three coin trick. It is said that he made quite a fair living from it!

His death was reported in December 1895.

CHAPTER SIX

PUNCH DOWSETT

Punch Dowsett was born in the year 1850. By trade he was a cordwainer, but later when he became unemployed he was taken on by Ted Napper, who finding the lad to be an apt pupil, put the finishing touches to his fistic education.

Although only 5ft. 2in. in height and scaling well under 8st., he entered in C. Frank's 9st. 7lb. competition on February 16th, 1875. He won the competition by defeating J. Browne, Tim Harrington, and Jem Laxton.

In July of the same year he won a silver cup and £5 at Hackney Wick, open to the world at 9st. In this he defeated Ben Stocking and Young Cable to win the competition.

Five months later he entered a 9st. 4lb. competition and defeated in the early stages Dick Longman, B. Ellis, and Savage. But in the final against Bill Green the judges could not separate them after four rounds, and a draw was declared. A week later they met in a renewal of the final, and this time Dowsett gained the decision.

He now met Harry Ross in an endurance bout and after contesting fifteen rounds in sixty-two minutes, won a £20 silver cup.

In March 1877, he gained another success when he entered an open 8½st. competition, defeating Bob Laxton and James Muskett.

On October 22nd, 1877, he won Bill Hundreds' Championship Featherweight Competition at 9st., defeating W. Steadman in the final.

Dowsett now entered into an endurance bout with the Featherweight Title at stake, his opponent being Tom Hawkins. Bill Hundreds was again the promoter and the venue was at Hoxton.

There was only ½lb. difference in their weights, Dowsett being the heavier at 7st. 10lb.

For over twenty-two rounds the two little gamecocks fought fiercely, with neither man gaining the advantage. Then towards the end of the 23rd round, Hawkins was sent staggering back from a heavy punch.

In the following round Dowsett did not follow up his advantage and allowed his opponent to recover, who after a while began to fight back as fiercely as ever.

In the 28th round, Dowsett after first landing his left on the chin, brought his right over with tremendous force to Hawkins' jaw, dropping him in a heap. Tom arose instantly and fought back well, but his blows lacked power. Once again Dowsett sent him to the floor, but again the game fellow got up and fought back, but was sent down for the third time. Once more he got to his feet but was sent down again. As Dowsett came in for the kill Tom caught him with a stinging punch to the nose, that brought the blood out in streams. Dowsett backed his man into a corner, but Hawkins fought back in furious fashion. He was, however, knocked down by a blow to the jaw, the bell coming to his rescue.

To the amazement of the spectators Hawkins was first up; in fact Dowsett had temporarily punched himself out. Tom led off and missed, Dowsett countering with two punches to the jaw, again sending the brave Hawkins to the floor.

The fighting of both men fell off and there were long spells of tedious sparring. Dowsett made no effort to force the fighting, allowing his opponent ample time to recover from the hammering he had received.

At the expiration of forty rounds the referee Mr Watson declared that as it was now twelve o'clock, he must stop the contest. The battle had lasted two hours and forty minutes. As neither party desired to fight the following day, the stakes were drawn, Dowsett retaining his title.

In 1878, Dowsett was defeated for the first time by Tommy Orange over six rounds. This solitary defeat bringing his career to a close.

CHAPTER SEVEN

DENNY HARRINGTON

Denny Harrington was born in the city of Cork, in Ireland on December 13th, 1849.

He became a pupil of Ted Napper, and it was as Napper's novice that he made his debut to the roped arena in a 10st. 7lb. competition, which took place in February 1872. In the preliminary rounds he defeated Jimmy Price and Harry Holden, but was unfortunate in coming up against Bat Mullins in the final, losing to the old champion on points over three rounds.

In another competition held in March of the same year, he was outpointed by Charley Davis in the final.

Denny was then matched in a bare knuckle contest against Jem Goode; the fight coming off at Long Reach. After a contest lasting one hour and forty minutes, the Irishman was awarded the victory.

He became great friends with Charley Davis who had recently won the Middleweight Title, and the two toured the country giving sparring exhibitions. Unfortunately Davis had to relinquish his title due to ill-health, and Harrington claimed the championship. By the September of 1876 he had established his claim, there being no one willing to fight him.

In the same year George Rooke the reigning American Middleweight Champion came over to this country, and soon after his arrival a match was arranged between him and Hugh Burns, the result being a draw after a contest lasting one hour and twenty minutes.

Overtures were now made for the two champions to meet for the Middleweight Championship. Eventually all the arrangements were satisfactorily concluded, and for the first time the champions of the Old and New World met for the 11st. title under Marquis of Queensbury Rules.

Although Harrington had a weight advantage of 3lb., at 10st. 13½lb., he was 4in. the shorter man.

As soon as they were within range, Rooke shot out his left hand, but

Harrington received the blow on his left arm. After a spell of cautious sparring they closed and fought two-handedly in a long rally. Denny bored his man to the ropes where he landed his left on George's nose, followed by a right cross that got home on the ear.

Another rally ensued by the ropes, Rooke accidentally striking Jack Baldock who was hovering there. In the exchange George managed to land only one effective punch, a left-hander. The fighting was fast and furious and soon Rooke began to display signs of weakness. Denny pressed forward and crossed his opponent with a right to the ear, followed by a punch on the nose, and again on the side of the head, knocking him down. George got up but before they could resume fighting, "Time" was called.

Rooke was slow in coming up, but as soon as they were within range, stood toe to toe with his opponent, both punching away furiously, all science forgotten. Denny once more landed that right cross to the ear, but was countered on the same spot by his adversary. Both were winded by their exertions, Harrington being the first to recover. He shot out a straight left that landed on his opponent's nose. This riled the American champion who fought his man to the ropes, where a regular scramble took place. Rooke went weak again and Denny lashed out with a left-hander that landed on the chin, but was countered by his opponent. They indulged in half-arm hitting, but the punches were ineffectual. As Harrington backed away rapidly Rooke chased after him, striking his man on the back of the head.

Rooke led off at the mark; a rally immediately following in his corner. After they broke away Harrington fought his man to the ropes, but received a left-hander on his left eye. The English champion retaliated with two heavy punches to his opponent's chin and ear. They clinched, then punched away, Denny's blows being the more effective. Towards the end of the round both men were showing signs of weakness, although Harrington did get home heavily to the mark and chest. Rooke struck his foe several times to the body but his punches lacked power, and the indications were at this stage that the English champion was going to win.

Both were showing the effects of the heavy fighting, but as soon as they neared each other, they commenced slogging away. Denny landed one heavy punch to George's chest, the latter missing with his counter. Harrington landed a light left to Rooke's eye, but was countered by a punch to the ribs. The English champion concentrated his attacks to Rooke's body, while the latter succeeded in landing a punch to Denny's chin. A fierce rally followed in Harrington's corner; Rooke connecting with a fine cross counter, and he forcèd his man to the ropes, but left himself open to a pile-driver to the stomach. Just as the round ended Rooke crossed his man again.

c

They sparred for about forty seconds before Denny landed his left to Rooke's nose, following it up with a right-hander to the ear. George fought back and succeeded in landing a flush hit on Harrington's nose. The latter forced Rooke into a rally and definitely got the better of the exchanges. Jack Baldock pushed his man into Rooke, the incident causing a tremendous commotion in which the referee and timekeeper were jostled about. In the midst of the general scramble both men went down, Harrington being bitten on the wrist by one of Rooke's supporters! Denny showed the injury to the referee but as he had been unsighted at the time, he ordered the fight to be continued.

On facing each other they sparred for some thirty seconds, then clinched and held, meanwhile both punching away weakly with their free hand. Harrington was the first to recover and crashed home a heavy right-hander that landed on his opponent's cheek. The American champion was forced back on the ropes, where he lay utterly prostrated. The ten seconds were tolled off but Rooke was unable to get up. Harrington was then declared the winner of a contest that had lasted twenty-two minutes and forty seconds. So Denny became the first undisputed World Middleweight Champion.

Harrington following this hard contest had a lengthy rest before defending his titles against Florrie Barnet. The setting was rather an unusual one for a championship fight, it being held under a railway arch in Bermondsey Street, lit by gas lights. The management of the affair being put into the hands of Mickey Rees, who did his best to keep the company as select as possible.

From the outset Harrington forced the fighting, dashing out his left to the neck, before they both got home with right-handers to the ribs. Denny again led off with his left to the neck, but was cross-countered to the jaw. A slashing rally followed, the men using both hands to good effect, Harrington getting the better of the exchanges. After breaking away the champion set about Barnet with great determination, landing left and right, and occasionally getting home to the stomach. Florrie did manage to connect with a good left-hander to Denny's right eye, drawing the blood. Harrington now brought his right round with great force, a grand rally following; Denny landing one punch full in the face, and another to the ribs.

The champion was eager to begin but Barnet was slow in coming up. Harrington dashed out his left, but was countered by a punch to his sore eye. Denny set about his man, and using both hands to good effect punched his opponent all over the ring. After two minutes and ten seconds of the round had passed, Denny landed a swinging left-hander to Barnet's jaw, and then sent a right-hander to the other side of the jaw, knocking him out of time.

In November of 1879, a match was hastily arranged between Harrington and Alf Greenfield of Birmingham. Although advertised as a fight for the Middleweight Title, Denny weighed in at 12st.! He had only done about five days training. Greenfield scaled 10st. 10lb.

From the start Greenfield took the lead, his left-hand work being particularly effective. Denny due to his lack of condition was content to stay on the defensive, relying on his right-hand punching to bring him victory. Earlier in the fight, however, his right-handers were inaccurate and fell short.

It was not until the 6th round that Harrington took the initiative, landing right and left heavily. Greenfield fought back and there were some warm exchanges; both were weak from their exertions as the round ended.

Greenfield was the first to recover and he continued to build up a big lead; Denny missing repeatedly with his upper-cuts.

In the 10th round Harrington seemed to regain his strength and there were some heavy exchanges. By round twelve both were weak after a bustling round, in which the lead alternated between the two.

Denny once more went on the defensive; by this time his eye was closed and Greenfield was looking confident of victory.

Harrington, however, made another recovery in the 14th round and made a great effort to turn the battle in his favour, but Greenfield gave back punch for punch.

In the 16th round Denny rallied again and took the earlier part of the round, but he then weakened and Alfred came on strong and took the round.

Harrington now steadily weakened allowing his opponent to land his punches as and when he pleased.

When the 18th round opened Denny dashed at his man and lashed out right and left, forcing Alf into a corner. The Brum fought back and had the better of the exchanges that followed. Harrington went on the retreat with Greenfield following; Denny then tripped over Alf's right foot. Instead of allowing his opponent time to put himself into a fighting attitude, Denny was no sooner on his feet before Greenfield drove him back to the ropes. Here Alf knocked his man backwards onto the top rope. The champion lay there suspended quite unable to rise, with his body half out of the ring, and whilst in that position Greenfield struck him twice. An appeal for a foul was made, and the referee immediately declared in favour of the champion; Greenfield throwing away the fight when victory was within his grasp. The contest had lasted one hour and ten minutes.

Harrington's next fight should have been against Tug Wilson, in May 1880, but the latter forfeited the stakes of £200.

Then in December of the same year Denny was matched with

William Sheriff of Leicester, for the Middleweight Title. On this occasion Harrington took great pains over his preparation. If anything he overdid it, for he was 5lb. inside the stipulated weight of 11st., 3lb. lighter than his opponent.

The story of this contest and how Harrington lost his championship, can be found in the chapter on William Sheriff.

Denny retired and became a stevedore, and he did nothing in the way of boxing at all. Then in 1900 there was some talk of him being matched against another veteran boxer, Barney Scannell, but this match fell through.

Harrington died in January 1911, aged sixty-one.

CHAPTER EIGHT

JOHN KNIFTON
'The 81-Tonner'

John Knifton holds a unique place in the history of British boxing, for he was the first professional Heavyweight Champion of England under Marquis of Queensbury Rules. He was also the first Scottish-born boxer to win the Heavyweight Title — in fact the only one to have done so in over a hundred years.

Knifton was born in the village of St. Cyrus, Kincardineshire on January 22nd, 1855. Some time later his family moved to the Kingsland area of London. In the neighbouring parish of Shoreditch, Ted Napper the former Featherweight Champion, ran his public house and sparring saloon in Nichol Street. It was here that Knifton received tuition from the old master. John was a big man standing 6ft. 1½in., and it was his size rather than skill that brought him to the fore in that establishment.

In May 1877, he entered a 'World Heavyweight Championship Competition' for a silver cup, defeating Jem Madden by a knockout in the 2nd round, Walter Watson by a knockout in the 1st round, and in the final outpointed Tom Tully over three rounds to gain the title.

Shortly afterwards he received a challenge from the ex-amateur Tom Scrutton to fight for the title in an endurance battle. A purse of £25 was offered and the bout was arranged for August 29th, 1877.

Scrutton was now a veteran of thirty-two, and was giving away ten years to his youthful adversary. He was also the shorter man by 5¼in. He did, however, have a weight advantage of 12lb., scaling 15st.

When "Time" was called neither man wasted any time in sparring. They instantly came together and commenced to bang away at each other. At this style of fighting Knifton was clearly superior, and by the 3rd round Scrutton was a beaten man. For round after round the game veteran was sent up, only to be knocked all over the ring. Knifton, however, seemed unable to put his man away.

In the 9th round fighting broke out among the spectators and the whole place was soon in an uproar. The proprietor fearing for his property, turned out the gas lights and the whole place was plunged into darkness! When eventually the lighting was restored, it was found that the referee Mr J. Jenn had left the building in the confusion. When the men met on the following day it was proposed that the fight should be renewed, but Scrutton refused knowing that any further meeting would lead to his inevitable defeat. The stakes were therefore awarded to Knifton.

John now entered into a bare knuckle contest against Jack Massey, who was at least 4st. the lighter man. After fighting for forty-one minutes the proceedings were halted by the police, and the stakes were eventually drawn.

Tom Allen the former American champion was in this country and he challenged Knifton for his title. Big John himself was willing enough but he could not get the required backing, and so had to forfeit his title.

Soon after this Knifton left for America where he had family connections, and stayed there several years.

On his return to this country he entered Billy Madden's £1,000 Heavyweight Championship Competition, where in the December of 1882 he was defeated over three rounds by Cod Middings, in one of the preliminary rounds.

On January 3rd, 1883, he drew with Roger Wallis over three rounds. Later in the same year he met Charlie Mitchell in an exhibition match lasting five minutes. John was completely outclassed by the new champion, who hammered him from one side of the ring to the other.

Efforts were made to get up a match with Jem Smith, but all attempts to bring the fight off were abortive.

His last ring appearance was in February 1887, in a catchweight competition, where in the final he was beaten on points by Toff Wall over three rounds.

Now at the age of thirty-three he decided to quit the ring, but did not enjoy a long retirement, for on May 6th, 1896, the ex-champion died aged forty-one.

CHAPTER NINE

TOMMY ORANGE

Tommy Orange was born in the Bethnal Green area of London on October 9th, 1856. From a very early age he started frequenting the sparring saloons in his vicinity, run by such men as Ted Napper and John Fleming. Fleming at that time was landlord of the 'Five Inkhorns', and Tommy was a regular visitor there.

At the age of sixteen he weighed, in his working clothes, about 7st. 6lb. One day Fleming called the lad to one side and offered him a fight against Panto for £1 a-side! Orange accepted eagerly and on the day appointed a small party of sportsmen made their way to a quiet spot on the Hackney Marshes. There was no ring nor ropes, the sportsmen themselves formed the enclosure in which the boys fought.

From the outset both lads went at each other like tigers. Panto proved to be a strong boy and as hard as nails. In one of the earlier rounds Tommy knocked his opponent clean off his legs with a right-hander, but in doing so broke the knuckle of his little finger. For an hour after this accident the fight continued, Orange only using his right hand for the occasional dig to the body. He punched away at Panto's head with the left hand and at the expiration of one hour and fifteen minutes, his opponent was compelled to give in.

The contest was reported in *The Sporting Life*, and there it stated that Tommy was a pupil of Ted Napper, which was not true. Napper made it his business to find the youth and the outcome was that Orange did join Ted's boxing academy. Under the tuition of the old champion Tommy's knowledge of boxing improved rapidly.

In May 1878, he was matched against George Hughes for £6 a-side, and the affair came off at Grays in Essex. On this occasion Tommy scaled 8st., Hughes being slightly the heavier man. With Ted Napper seconding him Orange gained his second victory after fighting for one hour and twenty minutes.

At that time Punch Dowsett and Tommy Hawkins were contenders for the Featherweight Championship, but Tommy defeated both men in six-round bouts held at the 'Blue Anchor' Shoreditch.

On his prodigy's behalf Napper challenged 'Beaky', a pugilist who had a tremendous reputation as a rough fighter; but in the four rounds that they fought, Tommy completely outclassed his opponent. As there was no stake money involved this can only be classed as an exhibition bout. His defeat of 'Beaky', however, had the effect of frightening away all the opposition, and it was quite a considerable time before Orange could get fixed up with a regular match. He was, however, kept extremely busy in Napper's sparring saloon, and was instrumental in attracting a number of people to Ted's establishment. The old champion was not over-endowed with money, which was why Tommy was not matched for more lucrative purses.

An example was his next engagement against Jack Donovan of Chelsea, the stakes being only £1 a-side!

From the start Tommy concentrated his attack to the body, and the punishment he dished out in that area caused Donovan to break away. Very few boxers of his day could stand up to Orange's body punches, and Donovan was no exception. When he realized how badly hurt his opponent was, Tommy redoubled his efforts and half-way through the 3rd round the Chelsea man conceded that he was beaten.

George Davis agreed to meet Orange in a bout with the knuckles; the stakes being £5 a-side. Davis had a good reputation as a fist fighter, and a selected company of sportsmen gathered in Epping Forest. The ring was pitched at the rear of the 'Rising Sun'.

Davis was a strong and sturdily-built man, several pounds heavier than Tommy. He had a fair knowledge of wrestling, and used his physical advantages by giving Orange a couple of severe falls in the early part of the fight.

In the 4th round, Tommy took the initiative and was able to land his favourite punch, a right-hander to the mark, knocking Davis clean off his legs. Gallantly Davis fought back, but from time to time another of those pile-drivers would land on the target. After fighting for forty-eight minutes, Davis could no longer continue, and victory went once more to the Bethnal Green man.

At this period the acknowledged champion of the Bantamweights was little Jem Laxton. He and Tommy had sparred together on a number of occasions, and there was very little to choose between the two. Finally the two were matched, Laxton having an 8lb. weight advantage, scaling 9st. He was, however, six years the older man.

In this the final bout of his career Tommy showed his superiority by forcing Laxton to retire in the 3rd round. By this victory Orange proved himself to be the best of the 9st. boxers.

Orange now retired and became a successful wood merchant and an owner of trotting horses.

CHAPTER TEN

TED PRITCHARD

Ted Pritchard was born in Lambeth, London, in the year 1866. He was by nature a pugnacious youth and quite early on he was employed in a boxing booth run by Bob Webb. In this, the hardest school of boxing, he developed the skills which were later to take him to the top of his profession.

His first entry into the ring proper was when he entered a couple of competitions in South London, winning both. He then entered a competition at the 'Windsor Castle' in Plumstead, defeating George Ashley by a knock-out in the 2nd round, and Jack Casey also in the 2nd round.

He then entered Frank Hynde's 10st. 2lb. competition held at the Royal Aquarium in Wood Green. In the opening round he knocked out Dave Galvin in three rounds; and Dick Leary in two rounds. Dave Burke was the favourite for the competition, and Ted was opposed to him in the final. Although Burke fought as well as ever, he could not beat the new sensation, who won comfortably on points over four rounds.

At this period Pritchard was a beautifully-built athlete. Standing 5ft. 9in. and scaling about 10st., he looked formidable with his powerful neck, shoulders, and legs. His mode of fighting was to attack his man, setting up a relentless onslaught that eventually wore his opponent down.

In February 1889, he met Jim Hayes for £100 a-side at 10st. 4lb., the contest taking place at the Lambeth School of Arms in Paradise Street.

From the start the impetuous Pritchard attacked his opponent, and although he had to take several hard punches, he soon had Hayes reeling around the ring. His left-handers to the body being particularly effective.

The supporters of Hayes began swarming near the ropes and the uproar was tremendous. In the 2nd round the Lambeth man smashed his way through his adversary's guard and sent him to the floor.

In the 3rd round the rapidly-weakening Hayes was sent down again. This was too much for the beaten man's supporters who invaded the ring, bringing the fight to a close. Amid a bedlam of noise the referee Mr John Angle, besieged on all sides by the ruffians, declared that the fight was adjourned, but later quite rightly gave the decision to Pritchard.

By this victory Ted had proved himself to be a top-notcher and it was not long before he was matched with Alec Burns at 10st. 8lb. Again the Lambeth School of Arms was the venue, but this time the proceedings went off without a hitch.

Towards the end of the 1st round, Pritchard caught his man with a fearful crack on the jaw, from which he never recovered.

Burns was still groggy when he came out for the 2nd round and Ted wasted no time. A left-hand dig to the body was followed by a right to the jaw, that knocked Burns down and out!

Unfortunately like many boxers before and since, Ted started to live the high life. With plenty of money and 'friends' he contracted a particularly nasty illness. He was sent over to the Continent for treatment, and he seemed to make a good recovery. He once more buckled down to training and in 1890 he was matched against Alf Mitchell at 11st., for £200 a-side.

During the training, however, Ted became ill again and the fight was called off. On recovering, a fresh match was made with Mitchell.

Pritchard proved his well-being by disposing of the ex-guardsman in four rounds. No sooner was the verdict announced when into the ring jumped Jack Burke, who challenged Ted to a match for £1,000 a-side. Pritchard was willing enough and soon found backers prepared to put up £500 on his behalf.

On this occasion the Middleweight Title was at stake, and an eager crowd gathered at the Albany Club in Holloway to witness what promised to be an exciting contest.

Burke was a beautiful boxer and in the 1st round his left-hand work, and his evasive footwork was a joy to see. As the fight progressed, however, Pritchard succeeded in breaking through his guard, and it was a worried-looking Burke who went back to his corner.

During the interval the referee Mr George Vize examined the gloves, the seams of which had split, but as the padding was still secure, he allowed the fight to go on. Ted tore into his man with his usual ferocious attack, and although he was caught with one cracking punch to the eye, began to take a commanding lead.

By the 3rd round Burke had nothing to offer and the tireless Pritchard finished him off, to gain for himself the Middleweight Title.

Ever since the Hayes fight there had been ill feeling between Pritchard and Jem Smith, for the latter was one of the ruffians who had invaded the ring on that occasion. So it gave Ted the greatest of satisfaction when he and Smith were matched for £500 a-side, and the Heavyweight Championship. Many believed that Pritchard was foolish in fighting a man so much above his weight, but it was a well-known fact that Smith was but a poor glove fighter.

Eventually the venue was agreed — Jack Wannup's Gymnasium in New Cross. Here about fifty or so spectators gathered round the ring to witness the contest.

Smith was in splendid shape; he had obviously taken great pains to get himself into the best possible condition.

From the outset Smith forced the fighting, and Ted was taken out of his stride by the sudden unexpected attack. Three times in the first round Pritchard was knocked to the floor, and it did appear as if he had been a little too ambitious. After the minute's rest, however, Ted had made a good recovery. Instead of taking the fight to his adversary, he feinted with the left, and stepped to one side as Smith came charging in. Twice more he used the same manoeuvre before swerving to the left and meeting the big man's rush with a crushing left-hander to the body. Jem tried to disguise the fact that he was hurt, and rushed to close quarters. Here he held Ted round the body with one hand and hit away with the other. Bob Watson the referee tore the men apart. Smith awkwardly covered up and tried to get to close quarters; Pritchard hitting him back with both hands.

The mauling tactics were angering the Lambeth man, and twice both fighters went down together. Then towards the end of the round a slashing left to the mouth put Smith down.

With great coolness Pritchard avoided the clumsy rushes of his opponent, and began to inflict terrible punishment with his two-handed hitting. Jem was soon beaten and sagged to the ropes, clutching them to keep himself from going down. Pritchard got home with a left-hander to the chin, knocking his man down. At "Nine" Jem was up, swaying about on trembling legs. He feebly pushed out a left that landed on Ted's face, the latter countering with a crashing right-hander to the chin, that dropped Smith for the full count.

It was not until the following year that an adversary appeared who had any chance of extending the Lambeth man. This was Jem Hall of Australia who had recently arrived in this country. He was the reigning Australian Middleweight Champion, having beaten among others, Bob Fitzsimmons.

Pritchard and Hall came together in a six-round bout at the National Sporting Club; the result of which was a draw. They were matched again, this time with the English Middleweight Title at stake.

Ted had always been a confident boxer who had a great belief in his own abilities. But during the training for this fight doubts began to assail him. For the first time he began to worry about the possibility of defeat. What caused this change in personality? The belief was that it was due to his previous illness which unfortunately not only affects the physical condition of the recipient, but also his mental faculties.

After a great deal of squabbling the eventual venue was located in a racing stable situated on the Sussex Downs.

Both men were in splendid condition physically, but the contrast in their outward demeanour was noticeable. Hall was as cool as a cucumber, while Pritchard was edgy and fidgety as he waited for the start of the contest.

It soon became obvious that it was not the old Ted. He boxed like a novice leaving himself wide open. Hall must have suspected a trap for to begin with he did not take advantage of the openings offered to him. Pritchard did succeed in getting home with a left-hander to Jem's mouth that drew the blood. Hall on the advice of his corner had been boxing cautiously, but realizing that the English Champion was not as formidable as he had been led to believe, changed his tactics. He flashed out a left-hand to the face, Pritchard being short with his counter. Again and again that long left shot out and Ted had no answer to it.

In the 2nd round Pritchard fought a lot better. Jem became careless and as he stepped in to throw another left-hander, he was countered with a terrific right to the cheek, and down went the Australian! As Hall sat on the canvas listening to the count, the referee hustled into the ring and moved Ted away from his stricken foe. At "Nine" Jem arose, still shaken from that superb punch. Again Pritchard erred in his tactics by allowing Hall to get to close quarters and hold on until the end of the round. If this had been the old Pritchard the Australian would never have survived the round.

Hall recovered during the interval and proceeded to take Ted apart. The Lambeth man fought with tremendous courage, but was subjected to a thrashing.

The end came in the 4th round when a series of brutal body blows proved too much for Pritchard, who sank to the canvas utterly beaten.

Pritchard now took a long rest before accepting a challenge from Dick Burge in the November of 1894. On the face of it Burge had over matched himself, but he believed that Ted's fighting days were over.

At the weigh in, Burge scaled only 10st. to his opponent's 11st. 6lb.

To begin with both sparred cautiously till Pritchard let go with a right-hander which Burge dodged; Dick countering with a left-hander to the body. Soon after Burge got home with a stinging left-hander to Ted's eye. The lighter man's clever footwork and trickiness giving him a decided edge by the end of the round.

Pritchard began to force the fighting in something like his old style.

Burge, however, by nimble footwork contrived to make his opponent miss again and again, occasionally popping in with lefts and rights, keeping the Lambeth man on the move the whole time. Ted threw several savage right-handers but failed to connect with his slippery foe. They closed and when they broke away Dick succeeded in landing a left-hander. Pritchard led with his left but Burge side-stepped and countered with a right-hander to the jaw as Ted came in close. Pritchard, however, would not be denied and closed with his man; both slipping down. When they arose Ted rushed in and succeeded in getting home with a heavy punch under Dick's heart, following it with a terrific punch to the jaw, knocking Burge down. The latter quickly regained his feet but had to take another punch that landed on the same spot. Burge crashed to the canvas completely senseless!

This was an entirely different performance from the one against Hall, and it was hoped that Pritchard was now back to his best.

Only three weeks later a match was made with Frank Craig, with Ted's Middleweight Title on the line. Oddly it was only scheduled for ten rounds but a tremendous ovation greeted the two men when they made their appearance at the Central Hall in Holborn.

Craig sat in his corner coolly having the gloves put on, while Pritchard, looking somewhat pale, was listening to Charlie Mitchell's last minute instructions.

On facing his opponent Ted seemed strangely ill at ease. The coloured man leered at him and proceeded to leap in and out, feinting with his left to draw his man, but Pritchard jumped nervously back. They circled around one another for about half a minute. Then Craig stepped forward with the intention of releasing a blow, but again Pritchard jumped back. This was fortunate for Craig because as he came forward his foot slipped, and for that one moment he was at the mercy of his opponent. He recovered quickly and when Ted belatedly went after his foe, he was caught with a right to the temple, a blow that temporarily dazed the Englishman, who promptly clinched. On breaking away Craig put in a light upper-cut, before forcing his man to the ropes. A right-hander to the head severely shook Pritchard who raised both hands to protect his face. As he did so the coloured man connected with a half-arm upper-cut, that stretched Pritchard out. Dazedly he scrambled to his hands and knees, rolled over onto his side, and remained in that position until the ten seconds were tolled off. It was a most disappointing effort from the once invincible Lambeth man.

In the following May, Pritchard was matched again with Jem Smith for the English Heavyweight Title. At the weigh in Ted scaled 11st. 6lb., conceding about 22lb. to the East Ender.

Smith looked really fit and confident as he waited for the fight to commence, while Pritchard was anything but his old confident self.

After a few moments of cautious sparring, Ted drove his left into Smith's mouth, causing him to reel away. Then angrily Jem rushed at the Lambeth man and succeeded in smashing him between the eyes. Both stood toe to toe hitting away at each other with some tremendous punches. Pritchard sank in one vicious punch to the body and Jem showed signs of weakness. Ted followed up his advantage with a stinging left to the nose, followed by a right-hander to the jaw that knocked Smith down! He regained his feet and in a brief rally held his own, until once more weakening. Pritchard proceeded to hit away with lefts to the face and chest, until at the end of two minutes' fighting, Jem again hit the floor! He arose looking flushed and bleeding and Pritchard got home with a right-hander to the heart. Smith was now at Ted's mercy, then unaccountably the referee stepped between them and pulled them apart. This brief respite benefitted Smith who fought back well in the later stages of the round.

The Lambeth man had taken a lot out of himself in the previous round, and although he took the initiative and landed a smashing left to Jem's mouth, it appeared to have little effect. Jem realizing that the power was no longer in his opponent's punches, went after his man, and they became locked together. After separating, Smith got home with a left to the mark, followed by a crashing right to the ribs that sent Pritchard back.

Smith forced the weakening Pritchard to the ropes and pinned him there, with his body half out of the ring. Jem landed several punches to the body, some of which landed below the belt! When at last Ted did manage to free himself, he was a beaten man. As he staggered across the ring Smith crossed him with the right, and Ted fell between the middle and bottom ropes. Pritchard's back was on the outer edge of the platform, with the bottom rope between the back of the knee. Smith's supporters now manipulated the rope making it utterly impossible for the fallen man to rise, and then held him down by the shoulder to make doubly sure! Altogether he was down for fifteen seconds when the bell ended the round. The referee then declared that Smith was the winner! It was a pathetic piece of refereeing; Joe Steers was completely cowed by Smith's rowdy supporters, and failed in his duty towards the Lambeth man. Smith should certainly have been disqualified for striking his opponent below the belt, and when Jem's supporters held Pritchard down, the count should have been stopped until such time as the fallen man could get up unmolested.

Not surprisingly Pritchard retired after this fiasco, but he did not enjoy a long retirement, for he died at the age of thirty-seven on November 20th, 1903.

CHAPTER ELEVEN

WILLIAM SHERIFF
'The Prussian'

William Sheriff was born on August 1st, 1847, at Leicester. From an early age he took an active interest in the sport of boxing, and soon proved himself to be a thoroughly game man.

Details of his early fights are unfortunately sparse. He won his first contest by defeating Joe Barrows in thirty minutes. Jack Marshall was likewise beaten in forty minutes. Then he seems to have had some kind of family vendetta, for in his next three fights he defeated Fred Haughton in fifty minutes, George Haughton in three hours and thirty minutes, and Jack Haughton in thirty-four minutes! This was followed by a drawn contest with Davis.

Then at the age of thirty-three he was matched against Denny Harrington for the latter's World and English Middleweight Titles, the stakes being £50 a-side.

Sheriff did most of his training at Alf Greenfield's establishment, the 'Swan with Two Necks', in Livery Street, Birmingham. When they went to scale Sheriff weighed in at 10st. 10lb., and Harrington surprisingly light at 10st. 9lb. Both were in the pink of condition.

Neither man appeared anxious to start hostilities, 'The Prussian' eventually leading off open-handed by way of a feeler, Harrington countering with a punch to the ribs. Denny let go his left which Bill cleverly avoided by ducking. They sparred for an opening before the Leicester man jabbed the champion on the nose with a left-hander, followed up with a right to the body, making Harrington wince. Heavy exchanges followed in a short rally before Sheriff slipped down. When he regained his feet, he used both hands very effectively; Denny at this stage of the contest was taking things calmly.

Bill almost immediately led off with his left which was neatly stopped. A series of rallies ensued, Denny trying repeatedly to upper-cut his man but failing to connect. They exchanged punches in the centre of the ring until Sheriff's left hand got locked under Harrington's arm. They

47

broke away smiling as the round ended.

Denny was the first to get to work, landing a left to the face followed by a right to the body. In attempting another right-hander, however, his blow fell short. The champion continued to press his opponent and led off with the left, but was countered heavily on the nose, causing the blood to flow. This annoyed Harrington who recklessly let fly two-handedly at his adversary, gaining a definite advantage by the end of the round.

The Leicester man, urged on by his supporters, flashed out a left-hander, and then brought his right round heavily on the jaw. Denny merely smiled and let go with his own right hand, that landed on the chest. After a little sparring Sheriff feinted with his left, stepped back, and landed the same hand on the right ear of his opponent, causing it to bleed slightly. Harrington now lost his temper and hit out wildly with both left and right, but Bill defended cleverly, and getting the advantage of higher ground, sent in left and right to both sides of his opponent's face.

The champion was the first to lead off with a left to the nose, but Sheriff stepped forward and banged his own left to the nose, and a right to the side of the head. Harrington forced his man to the ropes where they became locked; mutually they broke away. On regaining the centre of the ring the Leicester man got home with a left followed by a right, and repeated the blows soon afterwards. At this stage of the contest Sheriff still looked fresh, but Harrington was showing signs of weakness.

Bill forced the fighting and there were frequent rallies; the Leicester man repeatedly getting home with his right to the jaw, and a left to the champion's right eye, which soon began to swell. Working Harrington into his corner, Sheriff delivered a straight punch to the sore eye, Denny countering with a swinging right-hander.

The champion attempted to take the initiative and there was some fierce give and take fighting. Sheriff cleverly avoided a right cross by stepping back, and before Denny could recover, came back with a left to the nose and a swinging right-hander to the left eye. As the round ended he landed a vicious left-hander to Denny's stomach.

'The Prussian' had by now established a clear lead, but Harrington once more tried to even up matters. He led off successfully two or three times, and made one or two determined rushes. In attempting another rush, however, he was met with a punch full in the face. A fierce rally followed, the Leicester man gaining the advantage, landing left and right to the champion's face.

Sheriff now fought his man all over the ring, and Harrington had little to offer by way of resistance.

Denny let go a left to the nose but was countered by a left-hander to the body, and a right to the side of the head. They sparred for wind and manoeuvred for an opening before Bill got home twice in succession, left and right without return. Harrington by sheer strength drove his man to the ropes, but they almost immediately separated. On regaining the centre of the ring the champion appeared weak, and the Leicester man was able to land his left-handers repeatedly to the face.

Harrington came up looking decidedly groggy, and Bill proceeded to knock him down several times with his heavy right-handers. Only with the greatest difficulty could the champion rise before the ten seconds were tolled off. Sheriff tried to finish his man off and twice more in the round sent Denny down. The police who had been in attendance from the start, now came forward and stopped the proceedings by uprooting the stakes, the fight being abandoned for the day. Forty-four minutes had elapsed.

That evening a meeting took place in which the referee insisted that the fight should be renewed, but the backers of Harrington, realizing that their man stood no chance of victory, refused to obey the referee's orders. The stakes were quite rightly awarded to the Leicester man.

Sheriff remained inactive for two years before meeting Alf Greenfield in an exhibition match over three rounds in Birmingham. Then under the management of Arthur Chambers he journeyed over to America. His weight by this time had shot up to about 12st. 7lb., well above the middleweight limit, and it was at the heavier weight that he fought his six bouts over there.

In October of 1883, he met Charlie Mitchell; the result being a draw over seven rounds; Mitchell on this occasion conceding 25lb.

In January 1884, Bill defeated G. W. Sawdrey at Toledo. Then followed his great fight with John Welch. They were in the ring for five hours and three minutes before a draw was declared! Only eight days after this gruelling fight he met Mike Cleary and suffered his first defeat, being knocked out in the first round. Dominick McCaffrey also outpointed him in Pittsburgh.

On May 8th, 1884, the thirty-six year old veteran had his final bout, losing to Jake Kilrain; the police stopping the bout in the 3rd round.

After a few years in retirement he began to suffer from leg trouble, which as time went on became progressively worse. He returned to England in 1892 and thanks to the support of his friends, he received the best of medical attention. The treatment he received, however, failed to rectify the problem, and he rapidly went into a decline, dying at a friend's house in London on June 4th, 1893.

D

CHAPTER TWELVE

TED WHITE

Ted White was not a boxer of the classic mould. His object in the ring was to hit his opponent as hard and often as he could. He was not, however, just an aggressive fighter, for his left hand work was the best among the middleweights and heavyweights of his time.

Although he was a long time associated with the Walthamstow area, he was not born there. He first saw the light of day in Westminster on a site where the London Coliseum now stands. His family moved to the East End of London, and it was in this rough district that he spent his childhood days. As a youngster he used to frequent the various sparring saloons, in particular the 'Wheatsheaf' situated in Clare Market, and the 'Blue Anchor' at Shoreditch; so he had many opportunities of improving his boxing skills.

By trade he was a printer in a well-known publishing firm, and it was about this time that he joined the Belle Sauvage Athletic Club.

In the amateur championships of 1887, he had intended to enter the 10st. class, but was found to be overweight. He therefore entered the heavyweight section and became the lightest man ever to win the championship, defeating in turn, Trooper Cook and Jack Varley of Birmingham.

He decided to become a professional and entered Ben Hyam's 10st. competition, but was defeated by Jem Kendrick of Lambeth.

The Pelican Club had now been established in the Haymarket, and Ted's first contest there was against Pat Condon, whom he defeated in eight rounds. He then entered a competition there, defeating Bill Husband and pocketing the £15 prize-money.

White entered a series of competitions and was successful in winning Frank Hynde's 10st. 4lb. championship, beating Jack Richardson in the final. In a similar championship competition run by Charlie White, he was defeated by Sam Baxter of Islington in the final. His greatest success in 1889 was the winning of Frank Hynde's 11st. 4lb. competition, defeating the great Bat Mullins in the final.

Arthur Bobbett who had been defeated in one of the earlier rounds of the competition by Mullins, challenged his conqueror again but the latter was not interested having now retired. A similar challenge to White was accepted, and a twelve-round bout was soon arranged between the two.

In a slashing fight Ted knocked out his rival in the 9th round.

Tom Meadows of America was White's next opponent, and the match came off at Kennington. Meadows was one of those rough and ready fighters, and immediately the fight started proceeded to hurl a fusilade of punches at the Walthamstow man, who was kept very much on the defensive. By the 2nd round, however, Ted had weighed up his man, and stood boldly up to him, banging his solid left hand into Meadows' face with considerable force. It was a beautifully-timed blow but it failed to stop the Yankee. White now went in for in-fighting and fought at such a pace that Meadows could not keep up with it. The American, riled at his inability to land any effective punches, commenced boring in, holding and hitting his adversary. All orders to "Break away" were ignored by Meadows, and Ted had to fight his way free.

The American realizing that he could not defeat White by fair tactics, now started to fight dirty, and committed every foul in the book except biting! This state of affairs went on for two rounds. Ted finding himself roughly used, fought savagely at close quarters.

The end came in the 7th round when Meadows, outfought at all points, rushed his man to the ropes, and whilst holding him with one hand, butted White repeatedly. This was too much for the referee who had shown great leniency up to this point, and he promptly disqualified the American.

Victories over Alec Burns and Ted Rich followed, but then came a set-back when he was knocked out by John O'Brien, who later went on to win the Middleweight Title.

Ted's first match at the National Sporting Club was against Jack Welland, whom the Walthamstow man outpointed over twelve rounds.

He was offered a match against Billy McCarthy of Australia, one of the leading middleweights of the world at that time, but White found him far too formidable a foe at this stage of his career, and was compelled to cede victory after fighting thirteen rounds.

At this time the National Sporting Club were trying to arrange a Middleweight Title bout between John O'Brien and Ted Pritchard. But O'Brien contracted an illness that put him out of boxing for a couple of years, and Pritchard was not interested in fighting at this time. So the N.S.C. decided to put up the Middleweight Belt in a competition between eight selected men.

In the first series, White easily defeated Harry Holdsworth of St. Luke's. His second opponent was George Chrisp of Newcastle, and this proved to be a really good scrap, with Ted getting the decision. In the final he met Alf Bowman, also a former A.B.A. Heavyweight Champion, but the issue was never in doubt and White was presented with the English Middleweight Championship Belt.

George Chrisp issued a challenge to Ted to fight over the full championship distance of twenty rounds, and the pair were matched at the N.S.C.

In this bout White fully demonstrated his superiority over the Newcastle man, who never gave up trying, the contest going the full twenty rounds.

The Walthamstow man rested for eight months before he was called upon to meet another former A.B.A. Heavyweight Champion, Anthony Diamond. It was by far White's toughest fight, for Diamond was Ted's equal in cleverness and ring craft. White had to battle hard all the way, carrying the fight to his opponent. He was countered heavily on occasions, but he persevered with his aggressive tactics, and justly earned the decision after fighting the full twenty rounds.

Kid McCoy had recently arrived in this country and was trying to get a match against Dan Creedon of New Zealand; but instead was offered a bout against White, with the promise that should he win, he would be given further fights. Although at this time McCoy was an unknown quantity, he was supremely confident in his ability to defeat anybody in the world. The bout between McCoy and White was at 11st. 2lb., and of ten rounds duration, two minutes each round.

In the opening rounds McCoy took an early lead, his hooks and swings troubling Ted, but the latter eventually got that brilliant left hand of his working well, and he repeatedly jabbed his man. McCoy tried clinching, but White, with both hands free, hit out hard and often, and the American was glad to break away.

It was not a great fight to witness, as McCoy, finding himself up against it, indulged in hugging and smothering tactics; White eventually winning comfortably on points.

His final bout was against Dido Plumb at the N.S.C. The weight on this occasion being 11st. 4lb.

While the fight lasted it was full of interest, but in the 16th round White landed a right to the jaw that knocked Plumb out.

Now aged twenty-nine, Ted decided to retire, and soon afterwards became landlord of the 'Old Justice' in Southwark Bridge Road, which he ran with his wife for a number of years.

CHAPTER THIRTEEN

THE WORLD MIDDLEWEIGHT CHAMPIONSHIP

The Middleweight Division was established in this country in the year 1786, when 'Gentleman' Richard Humphries defeated the famous Jewish pugilist Daniel Mendoza.

If one were to compute the average weight of all the champions of this class since then, the answer would be somewhere in the region of eleven stone. There were a couple of champions who scaled less than this, but they were exceptional fighters of the highest class, namely Jack Randall and Ned Turner.

So to qualify as a middleweight titular affair, one of the contestants must weigh somewhere in the region of 154lb.

Originally for a contest to be regarded as a World Championship, the fighters had to be champion of the 'Old World', i.e. England, and the champion of the 'New World', i.e. America.

The first contest so recorded was the one which took place between Tom Sayers and John C. Heenan, for the World Heavyweight Championship, in April 1860. Both men were the respective champions of England and America.

It is these criteria of eligibility and weight which must be used in establishing who the earlier world champions were.

In America the first claimant to the title is sometimes given as Tommy Chandler, who defeated the Englishman Dooney Harris. The weights were Chandler 9st. 10lb., and Harris 9st. 11lb. Too low to qualify as middleweights. Neither was Harris the best of the English 10st. pugilists.

The next claimant to the title was George Rooke, the younger brother of the more famous Jack. George had been born in Dundalk, Ireland, and in 1862 at the age of twenty-three, went to America. Three years later he had his first recorded fight, defeating Tim Hussey in thirty minutes. In his next contest against George Collins, he was definitely getting the better of the battle, when the decision was given against him on a disputed foul. He then fought Rocky Moore for the American

Middleweight Title, but lost after a severe contest lasting one hour and five minutes. Rooke challenged Moore to a return bout but the latter declined, and retired from the ring. Over the next few years George established himself as the American Champion by his defeats of Tim Hussey, Jack Smith, and Roger Colne.

In 1876, Rooke returned to England, and was quickly matched against Hugh Burns. This fight took place at Newmarket and resulted in a draw, after the men had been fighting for one hour and twenty minutes. A match was then made against the English Champion, Denny Harrington, at 11st.

Here are two adverts that appeared in *The Sporting Life* which makes it quite clear that in the contest between Harrington and Rooke, the World Middleweight Title was at stake.

> *November 17th, 1877.* "George Rooke (The American Champion) made challenge to the world at 10st. 12lb. for the Middleweight Championship and a £50 or £100 cup under Marquis of Queensbury Rules."

> *March 9th, 1878.* (i.e. 3 days before the contest) "March 13th, on which occasion George Rooke and Denny Harrington (Middleweight Champions of the World) will appear."

The result of the contest was a resounding win for the English Champion Denny Harrington, who became the first boxer to win the undisputed Middleweight Title. He twice successfully defended the title before losing it to the Leicester boxer, William Sheriff, on December 17th, 1880.

Sheriff never defended the title, and by 1883 had out-grown the division.

Charlie Mitchell was perhaps the best middleweight in the world at this time, but he was only interested in the premier title.

Mike Donovan's claim to the World Championship can be ignored. His victory by a two-round points decision over George Rooke in March 1881, completely overlooks the fact that Rooke had already been defeated by Harrington. In fact Rooke still claimed the American Title, and he defended this successfully by knocking out William C. McClellan on December 1st, 1881.

The next claimant to the title is perhaps the most ridiculous of all. George Fulljames of Canada is alleged to have claimed the title sometime in 1884, and was subsequently beaten by the nonpareil Jack Dempsey, supposedly for the title. Three months *before* fighting Fulljames, Dempsey had fought at 9st. 4lb. Nine months *after* his fight with Dempsey, Fulljames was defeated by Harry Gilmore for the Canadian Featherweight Title! So when Dempsey met Fulljames neither boxer could have exceeded 10st., and probably Fulljames was considerably lighter than this. So the Middleweight Title could not have been at stake.

Dempsey was certainly recognized as the champion by the Americans after defeating Jack Fogarty, George LaBlanche, and Johnny Reagan. But in a return fight with the Canadian LaBlanche in 1889, Dempsey was knocked out by a pivot punch, which was *afterwards* made illegal. Dempsey was still regarded by the Americans as the champion.

There is no doubt that at this period of time, the Australians had the best boxers in the Middleweight Division. It was by his defeat of Australian Billy McCarthy that Dempsey gained some international recognition as champion.

Then also from Australia came Bob Fitzsimmons, a veteran of ten years experience. He completely outclassed Dempsey to win the title, and gained universal recognition by defeating his former conqueror Jem Hall, and thrashing Dan Creedon of New Zealand, who was later to win both the English Middleweight and Heavyweight Titles.

This is how the **WORLD MIDDLEWEIGHT TITLE BOUTS** should appear in the record books:

1878 Mar 12 Denny Harrington W. ko 6 George Rooke (154lb.)   London
1879 May 26 Denny Harrington W. ko 2 Florrie Barnet   Bermondsey
1879 Nov 27 Denny Harrington W. f. 18 Alf Greenfield (168-150)   London
1880 Dec 17 William Sheriff W. 11r. 44m. Denny Harrington (152-149)
                                      Lapworth
1883   (Sheriff outgrew division)
1886 Feb 3   Non. Jack Dempsey W. ko 27 Jack Fogarty (USA)   New York
1886 Mar 4   Non. Jack Dempsey W. ko 13 George LaBlanche   Larchmont
1887 Dec 13 Non. Jack Dempsey W. ko 45r. 73m. Johnny Reagan Long Island
1889 Aug 27 George LaBlanche W. ko 32r. Non. Jack Dempsey   San Francisco
            (LaBlanche won the fight by use of a 'pivot' blow. It was
            later considered to be an illegal punch, and was
            subsequently barred. The Americans still recognised
            Dempsey as the champion)
1890 Feb 18 Non. Jack Dempsey W. pts. 28 Australian Billy McCarthy
                             San Francisco
1891 Jan 14 Bob Fitzsimmons W. ko 13 Non. Jack Dempsey   New Orleans
1893 Mar 3   Bob Fitzsimmons W. ko 4 Jem Hall (163½-167½)   New Orleans
1894 Sep 26 Bob Fitzsimmons W. ko 2 Dan Creedon (156-157)   New Orleans
1896   (Fitzsimmons relinquished title)
1896 Dec 26 Kid McCoy W. ko 9 Bill Doherty   Johannesburg
1897 Dec 17 Kid McCoy W. ret. 15 Dan Creedon   Long Island
            (McCoy competed among the heavyweights)

HEAVYWEIGHT TITLE FIGHTS

1877 May 19	John Knifton W. 3 Tom Tully	London
	(Final of Championship Competition)	
1877 Sep 3	John Knifton W. 9 Tom Scrutton (198-210)	London
	(Tom Allen returned to this country from America and it was expected that Knifton would accept his challenge but the latter was unable to get the necessary financial backing, and so forfeited his title)	
1877 Oct 29	Tom Allen W. 7r. 16m. 25s. Tomkin Gilbert	London
1878 Apr 4	Tom Allen W. f. 5r. 18m. 25s. Charley Davis	Cambridge Heath
1878 Apr 24	Jem Gaiger W. 3 George Rivett	Finsbury
	(Final of Championship Competition)	
1879 Apr 22	Tom Allen D. 25r. 100m. Jem Stewart (184-170)	London
1880 Feb 25	Alf Greenfield W. f. 20r. 83m. Jem Stewart	Chelsea
	(Greenfield claimed title)	
1882 Nov	(Allen retired)	
1882 Dec 22	Charlie Mitchell W. 3 Dick Roberts (143-149)	Mayfair
	(Final of Championship Competition)	
1883 Jun 29	Alf Greenfield W. 3 Jack Burke	Manchester
	(Final of Championship Belt Competition)	
	(Greenfield and Mitchell now left for America and were absent for several years. The outstanding boxer during this period was Charles 'Toff' Wall who in 1886 defeated the former champion John Knifton over 3 rounds in competition. Wall also outclassed Jem Smith in an exhibition match)	
1889 Mar 16	Alf Mitchell W. 4 — Bartlett	London
	(Final of Championship Competition)	
1889 Apr 25	Bill Goode W. ret. 1 Teddy O'Neil	Wood Green
	(Final of Championship Competition)	
1890	(Wall retired)	
1890 Feb 7	Charlie Mitchell W. 4 Jem Mace (Police)	Edinburgh
	(Boxing Championship of England) (2 Minute Rounds)	
1891 Jul 27	Ted Pritchard W. ko 3 Jem Smith	New Cross
1894	(Mitchell retired)	
1895 May 10	Jem Smith W. ko 2 Ted Pritchard (182-160)	Holborn
1895 Nov 26	Jem Smith W. dis. 9 Dick Burge	Clapham Junction
1896 Jan 27	Dan Creedon W. ko 2 Jem Smith (162-180)	N.S.C.
	(Creedon left country)	
1899 ?	Jack Scales W. 2 Jack Broderick	London
	(Final of Championship Competition)	
1900 Feb 22	Pat Daley W. ko 1 Jem Styles (55 sec.)	Wonderland
	(Final of Championship Competition)	

1901 Apr 1	George Chrisp W. ko 8 Ben Taylor (Native)	Gateshead
1901 May 20	Phil. Jack O'Brien W. ko 11 George Chrisp (Open)	Newcastle
1901 Jun 25	Phil. Jack O'Brien W. ko 6 Harry Neumier	Newcastle
1901 Nov 7	Phil. Jack O'Brien W. ko 1 Jack Scales	Liverpool
1901 Dec 13	Phil. Jack O'Brien W. dis. 4 Yank Kenny	—
1902 Jan 18	Phil. Jack O'Brien W. 4 Frank Kelly	Scotland
1902 Jan 20	Phil. Jack O'Brien W. 2 Pat McDonald	Scotland
1902 Feb 1	Phil. Jack O'Brien W. dis. 5 Yank Kenny	West Hartlepool
	(O'Brien returned to America)	
1902 Jun 25	Denver Ed Martin W. rsf 5 Sandy Ferguson (Open)	N.S.C.
1902 Jun 25	Jack Scales W. ko 10 Ben Taylor (Native)	London
	(Coronation Championship Belt)	
1902 Jul 25	Denver Ed Martin W. 15 Bob Armstrong	Crystal Palace
1902 Aug 16	Denver Ed Martin W. rsf 3 Frank Craig	Newcastle
1902 Aug 30	Denver Ed Martin W. ko 4 Frank Craig	Newcastle
	(Martin returned to America)	
1902 Oct 13	Jack Scales W. ko 7 Harry Slouch Dixon	—
1902 Nov 8	Charlie Wilson W. ko 3 Jack Scales	London
1903 Mar 16	Ben Taylor D. 13 Harry Slouch Dixon	Wonderland
1903 May 2	Jack Palmer W. ko 12 Ben Taylor	Newcastle
	(Palmer's claim to the title was weak, as both he and Taylor had been defeated by Jack Scales. Wilson's claim was the strongest, but he did not receive general recognition)	
1903 Jun 15	Frank Craig D. 12 Harry Slouch Dixon	Wonderland
1903 Jul 27	Jack Palmer W. ko 12 Frank Craig	Newcastle
	(Palmer went to South Africa)	
1904 Dec	Jack Scales D. 10 Mike Shallow	Newport
1905 Dec 18	Jack Palmer W. ko 4 Geoff Thorne	Newcastle
1906 Oct 29	Gunner James Moir W. f. 9 Jack Palmer	N.S.C.
1907 Feb 25	Gunner James Moir W. ko 1 Tiger Smith (169 sec.)	N.S.C.
1909 Apr 19	Iron Hague W. ko 1 Gunner James Moir (167 sec.)	N.S.C.
1910 Feb 11	P. O. Curran W. ko 15 Iron Hague	Plymouth
1910 May 23	P. O. Curran W. f. 2 Gunner James Moir	Mountain Ash
1910 Aug 5	P. O. Curran W. ko 2 Seaman Grant	Plymouth
1910 Aug 18	P. O. Curran W. ko 6 Jem Roche	Dublin
1910 Aug 31	P. O. Curran W. ko 1 Peter Rice	Plymouth
1910 Sep 26	P. O. Curran dnc 7 Jewey Smith (Belt)	Wonderland
1910 Oct 30	P. O. Curran W. ko 3 Jewey Smith	Plymouth
1910 Dec 12	P. O. Curran W. ret. 2 Gunner Hewitt	Plymouth
1911 Jan 30	Iron Hague W. ko 6 Bill Chase	N.S.C.
	(Despite his loss to Curran the N.S.C. still continued to recognize Hague as champion)	
1911 Apr	P. O. Curran W. ko 4 Jack Scales	Plymouth

1911 Apr 24   Bomb. Billy Wells W. ko 6 Iron Hague (Lonsdale Belt)   N.S.C.
(The legitimate champion Curran was ignored by the autocratic N.S.C., who nominated Hague, who had been defeated by Curran, and Wells who had been beaten by Gunner James Moir! Curran continued to claim the title, and was not beaten by a British-born boxer until December, 1912, when Dan Voyles defeated him on a disqualification. Voyles in turn was stopped by Packey Mahoney in 16 rounds, on March 17th, 1913, at the N.S.C. On June 30th, 1913, Bombardier Billy Wells knocked out Mahoney in 13 rounds to become the undisputed champion.)

LIGHT-HEAVYWEIGHT TITLE FIGHTS

1911 Feb 6   Bandsman Dick Rice W. f. 18 Tom Thomas (167-173) Wonderland
1914 Mar 9   Dick Smith W. 20 Dennis Haugh (Lonsdale Belt)   N.S.C.

MIDDLEWEIGHT TITLE FIGHTS

1872 Apr 15   Bill Brooks W. 5 Jem Stewart (155lb.)   Bow
     (Final of Championship Competition)
1872 Dec 11   (Brooks died)
1873 Jan 7   Charley Davis W. 14r. 88m. John McConnell (Bow Cup)   London
1873 Apr 21   Charley Davis W. 21r. 84m. Ted Napper (147-140) Grafton Chapel
1875 Jun 12   Jack Madden W. 3 George Hope (155lb.)   London
     (Final of Championship Competition)
1876 June   (Davis retired owing to ill health)
1876 Sep   (Denny Harrington claimed title and was generally recognized)
1878 Mar 12   Denny Harrington W. ko 6 George Rooke (153½-150)   London
1879 May 26   Denny Harrington W. ko 2 Florrie Barnet (163-161)   Bermondsey
1879 Nov 27   Denny Harrington W. f. 18r. 70½m. Alf Greenfield London District
1880 Dec 17   William Sheriff W. 11r. 40m. Denny Harrington (152-149)
     Marsden Green
1883   (Sheriff outgrew division)
1883 Feb 9   Jack Burke W. 3 Jack Massey   London
     (Final of Championsip Competition)
1887 Aug 30   Bill Goode W. 15r. Tom Lees (154lb.)   Lambeth
1888 Nov   Bill Goode W. 12 Arthur Bobbett (150-152)   Manchester
1889 Mar 16   Jem Burchell W. 5 Arthur Bobbett (154lb.)   Islington
     (Final of Championship Competition)
1889 Apr 25   Ted White W. 4 Bat Mullins (154lb.)   Wood Green
     (Final of Championship Competition)
1890 Feb 8   Charles 'Toff' Wall W. 12 Bill Goode   London
     (Wall retired)

1890	Ted Pritchard W. ko 4 Alf Mitchell (154lb.)	London
1891 Mar 12	Ted Pritchard W. ko 3 Jack Burke (154lb.)	London
1891 Dec 12	John O'Brien W. ko 8 Alf Mitchell (158lb.)	N.S.C.
1892 Aug 20	Jem Hall W. ko 4 Ted Pritchard (158lb.)	N.S.C.
	(Hall left country)	
1893 Mar 6	Ted White W. 4 Alf Bowman	N.S.C
	(Final of Championship Competition)	
1893 Apr 24	Ted White W. 20 George Chrisp (154lb.)	N.S.C.
1894 Jan 15	Ted White W. 20 Anthony Diamond	N.S.C.
1894 Oct 4	Frank Craig W. ko 2 John O'Brien	N.S.C.
1894 Nov 23	Frank Craig W. ko 2 Alf Mitchell	N.S.C.
1894 Nov 26	Ted Pritchard W. ko 2 Dick Burge	London
1894 Dec 17	Frank Craig W. ko 1 Ted Pritchard (158lb.)	London
1895 Oct 14	Dan Creedon W. 20 Frank Craig	N.S.C.
	(Creedon left country)	
1896 Jun 1	Ted White W. rsf 16 Dido Plumb (158lb.)	N.S.C.
	(White retired)	
1897 Oct 23	Dick O'Brien W. ko 2 Frank Craig (158lb.)	Birmingham
1897 Dec 31	Dick Burge W. f. 4 Dick O'Brien	Birmingham
1898 Feb 25	Anthony Diamond W. 12 Dido Plumb (158lb.)	Birmingham
	(Final of Championship Competition)	
	(Diamond retired)	
1898 Sep 5	Dick Burge W. ko 1 Arthur Akers	London
1898 Nov 25	Frank Craig W. ko 13 George Chrisp	Newcastle
	(Craig left country)	
1900 Feb 9	Dick Burge W. ko 1 Jack Scales	London
1900 Mar 19	Dido Plumb W. rsf 8 Jem Ryan (154lb.)	N.S.C.
1900 Oct 15	Charlie McKeever W. 15 Dido Plumb (Open) (154lb.)	N.S.C.
1901 Aug 19	Phil. Jack O'Brien W. ko 6 Dido Plumb (Open) (154lb.)	London
1901 Nov 18	Phil. Jack O'Brien W. f. 7 Frank Craig	N.S.C.
1901 Dec 9	Charlie McKeever W. 12 Jack Palmer	Newcastle
1902 Jan 27	Phil. Jack O'Brien W. f. 3 Charlie McKeever (Open)	London
	(O'Brien returned to America)	
1902 Jun 23	Jack Palmer W. ko 7 Dave Peters	Merthyr
1902 Jul 19	Jack Palmer W. 20 Eddie Connolly	Newcastle
1902 Aug 23	Jack Palmer W. rsf 7 Eddie Connolly	N.S.C.
1902 Nov 24	Jack Palmer W. 12 Eddie Connolly	N.S.C.
1903 May 25	Jack Palmer D. 15 Jack 'Twin' Sullivan	N.S.C.
	(Palmer outgrew division)	
1904 Oct	Jim Courtney W. 10 Jim Styles (154lb.)	Cardiff
	(Final of Championship Competition)	
1905 Feb 27	Charlie Allum W. rsf 10 Jack Kingsland	N.S.C.
1906 Mar 19	Pat O'Keefe W. 15 Mike Crawley (158lb.)	N.S.C.
1906 Apr 23	Pat O'Keefe W. ko 6 Mike Crawley (156lb.)	N.S.C.

1906 May 23	Tom Thomas W. 15 Pat O'Keefe	N.S.C.
1908 Apr 30	Tom Thomas W. ko 5 Mike Crawley	London
1908 Jun 1	Tom Thomas W. ko 4 Tiger Smith (158lb.)	N.S.C.
1909 Dec 20	Tom Thomas W. ko 2 Charlie Wilson (Lonsdale Belt) (160lb.)	
		N.S.C.

WELTERWEIGHT TITLE FIGHTS

1882 Apr 4	Charlie Mitchell W. 3 Ned Harnatty (147lb.)	Chelsea
	(Final of Championship Competition)	
1884 Apr 16	Johnny Robinson W. rsf 2 Arthur Cooper (144lb.)	Islington
	(Final of Championship Competition)	
1887 Jan 19	Alec Roberts Won Jack Donoghue (148lb.)	London
	(Final of Championship Belt Competition)	
1888 Jan 25	Alec Roberts Won Arthur Cooper (148lb.)	London
	(Final of Championship Belt Competition)	
1888 Sep 24	Alec Roberts D. 53r. Arthur Bobbett (147lb.)	Lambeth
1889 Mar 16	Sam Baxter W. 4 Ted White (144lb.)	London
	(Final of Championship Competition)	
1889 —	Ted White Won Jack Richardson (144lb.)	Pelican Club
	(Final of Championship Competition)	
1890 ?	Anthony Diamond W. ko 10 Arthur Bobbett (148lb.)	—
1891 Mar 11	Harry Nickless W. ko 6 Johnny Robinson (144lb.)	Ormonde Club
1892 Jan 27	Dick Burge W. ko 2 Lachie Thompson (138-144)	London
1895 Jan 25	Dick Burge W. ko 4 Tom Williams	N.S.C.
1897 Jan 28	Dick Burge D. 10 Eddie Connolly (Police) (146lb.)	Birmingham
1897 May 31	Tom Causer W. f. 7 Dick Burge (133-142)	London
1897 Oct 8	Dick Burge W. ko 1 Tom Causer	London
1897 Dec 12	Bobby Dobbs W. ret. 8 Dick Burge (Open) (133-143)	London
1899 Feb 22	Bobby Dobbs D. 1 Joe McDonald (Police) (144lb.)	Glasgow
1899 Mar 14	Bobby Dobbs W. ko 2 Joe McDonald	Gateshead
1902 Jan 22	Tom Woodley W. ko 14 Jem Styles (Native) (146lb.)	Newcastle
1902 Sep 15	Tom Woodley W. pts. 11 Eddie Connolly (Open) (144lb.)	London
1903 Jan 26	Eddie Connolly W. 15 Tom Woodley (Open) (146lb.)	N.S.C.
	(Connolly left country)	
1903 Nov 16	Charlie Allum W. ko 9 Charlie Knock (Native) (146lb.)	London
1904 Jan 4	Peter Brown W. 6 Jack Kingsland (Belt) (Native) (148lb.)	London
1904 Feb 1	Charlie Knock W. 12 Charlie Allum (Native)	London
1904 Feb 15	Jack Clancy W. 15 Pat Daley (Open)	N.S.C.
1904 May 2	Jack Clancy W. 10 Peter Brown (Belt) (144lb.)	Wonderland
1904 May 14	Jack Clancy W. 20 Bobby Dobbs (144-140)	Newcastle
1904 Jun 4	Jack Clancy W. ko 3 Charlie Allum (146lb.)	Newcastle
1904 Oct 9	Jack Clancy D. 20 Bobby Dobbs (146lb.)	Newcastle
	(Clancy left country)	
1905 Feb 20	Tom Woodley W. f. 5 Charlie Knock (144lb.)	Wonderland
1906 May 21	Charlie Knock W. rsf 17 Curley Watson (144lb.)	London

1906 Nov 25	Curley Watson W. 10 Andrew Jeptha	Wonderland
1906 Dec 17	Curley Watson W. 10 Charlie Knock	London
1907 Feb 11	Curley Watson W. 20 Andrew Jeptha (144lb.)	Wonderland
1907 Mar 25	Andrew Jeptha W. ko 4 Curley Watson	Wonderland
1907 Aug 8	Joe White W. 15 Andrew Jeptha	Merthyr
1907 Nov 18	Curley Watson W. 15 Andrew Jeptha	N.S.C.
1908 Apr 18	Curley Watson W. 10 Charlie Knock (Belt) (148lb.)	London
1908 May 21	Joe White W. 20 Curley Watson	Liverpool
1908 Nov 23	Johnny Summers W. rsf 14 Jack Goldswain (134-144½)	N.S.C.
1909 Aug 21	Andrew Jeptha W. f. 7 Joe Heathcote	Wigan
1910 Feb 23	P. O. Roche W. 20 Dick Lee	King's Hall
	(Final of Championship Competition)	
1910 Mar 3	Joe White D. 15 Bobby Dobbs	Hull
	(White outgrew division)	
1910 Mar 21	Young Joseph W. f. 11 Jack Goldswain (147lb.)	N.S.C.
1911 Jan 23	Arthur Everden W. f. 3 Young Joseph	"The Ring"

LIGHTWEIGHT TITLE FIGHTS

1872 Apr 16	Bat Mullins W. 5 Jack Ward (Bow Cup) (128lb.)	Soho
	(Final of Championship Competition)	
1875 Jan 12	Lumpy Hughes W. 3 Tom Hooker (140lb.)	London
	(Final of Championship Competition)	
1876 Mar 18	Bob Habbijam W. 3 Jem Laxton (140lb.)	Islington
	(Final of Championship Competition)	
1877 Mar 30	W. (Soldier) Robinson W. ko 3 Jem Laxton (140lb.)	Sadler's Wells
	(Final of Championship Competition)	
1878	(Mullins outgrew division)	
1880 ?	Charlie Mitchell won Championship Competition.	
		'The Eagle', Finsbury
1883 Jun 29	H. Conley W. 3 G. Stevens	Manchester
	(Final of Championship Competition)	
1888 Nov 5	Johnny Robinson D. 12 Dick Burge (138lb.)	Newcastle
1889 Feb 23	Sam Baxter W. ko 1 Dave Galvin (134lb.)	London
	(Final of Championship Competition)	
1889 Feb 23	Bill Whately W. 4 Harry Mead (134lb.)	London
	(Final of Championship Competition)	
1889 Mar 16	Harry Denny won Championship Competition (134lb.)	London
1889 Apr 27	Bill Cheese W. 4 Arthur Gutteridge (140lb.)	London
	(Final of Championship Competition)	
1891 May 25	Dick Burge W. f. 11 Jem Carney	London
1891 —	Harry Nickless W. ko 9 Bill Hatcher (140lb.)	Clapham Junction
1894 ?	Harry Webster won Championship Competition (134lb.)	
		New Adelphi Club
1894 May 4	Dick Burge W. ko 28 Harry Nickless (140lb.)	London
	(Burge outgrew division)	

1894 Nov 22	Tom Causer W. ko 2 Tommy Askwith	Clapham
1895 Oct	Arthur Lock W. 3 Tom Ireland (134lb.)	London
	(Final of Championship Competition)	
1896 Dec 29	Tom Causer W. ret. 5 Maurice Greenfield (134lb.)	Birmingham
	(Final of Championship Competition)	
1897 Apr	Joe Anderson W. 6 Tom Ireland (134lb.)	Bethnal Green
	(Final of Championship Competition)	
1898 Mar 6	Tom Causer W. 10 Arthur Lock (134lb.)	Sheffield
1898 Apr 25	Johnny Hughes W. 20 Jem Curran (138lb.)	N.S.C.
1899 Mar 3	Tom Ireland Won George Cunningham (132lb.)	Wonderland
	(Final of Championship Belt Competition)	
1900 Jun 2	George Cunningham Won Bill Chester (128lb.)	Wonderland
1900 Aug 2	Tom Ireland W. 2 Jack Goldswain (132lb.)	Wonderland
1900 Sep 3	Jack Everhardt W. f. 10 Tom Ireland (Open) (140lb.)	Wonderland
1900 Nov 20	Jabez White W. ko 8 Harry Greenfield (128lb.)	N.S.C.
1901 Feb 11	Pat Daley W. ret. 12 Johnny Hughes (140lb.)	N.S.C.
1901 Feb 18	Jim Barry W. ko 9 Tom Dixon (132lb.)	Newcastle
1901 Feb 23	Ted Ware W. 8 Jack Fairclough (134lb.)	Wonderland
	(Final of Championship Competition)	
1901 —	Bill Nolan won Championship Competition (132lb.)	Wonderland
1901 Dec 23	Jabez White D. 20 Jem Curran	Birmingham
1902 Feb 26	Tommy Hogan W. ko 8 Bill Chester (Open) (128lb.)	N.S.C.
1902 Apr 21	Jabez White W. ko 6 Bill Chester (134lb.)	N.S.C.
1902 Jun 21	Jabez White W. 15 William 'Spike' Sullivan (134lb.)	N.S.C.
1903 Apr 20	Jabez White W. 15 William 'Spike' Sullivan	London
1905 Mar 6	Young Joseph W. 10 Dick Lee (Belt) (128lb.)	Wonderland
1906 Jan 8	Jabez White W. 15 Bob Russell (136lb.)	Birmingham
1906 Jan 29	Jack Goldswain W. ko 13 Fred Buckland (140lb.)	N.S.C.
1906 Mar 19	Johnny Summers W. 20 Arthur Hayes (128lb.)	N.S.C.
1906 Apr 24	Jack Goldswain W. 20 Jabez White (140lb.)	N.S.C.
	(Goldswain outgrew division)	
1908 Apr 1	Joe Fletcher W. ko 7 Jack Ward (135lb.)	N.S.C.
1909 Nov 9	Freddie Welsh W. 20 Johnny Summers (Lonsdale Belt)	N.S.C.

FEATHERWEIGHT TITLE FIGHTS

1872	Dick Goodwin presented with Championship Featherweight Belt. (Value 40gn.)	
1872 Dec 20	Young Hundreds presented with Championship Belt. (126lb.)	
1874 Sep 9	Bill Kennedy W. 3 — Purvey	London
	(Final of all-comer's competition)	
1877 —	Tom Jenkins won Champion's Cup Competition (122lb.)	London
1877 Oct 22	Punch Dowsett W. 3 W. Steadman (126lb.)	London
	(Final of Championship Competition)	
1877 Dec 11	Punch Dowsett D. 41r. 160m. Tom Hawkins	London
	(Dowsett retired)	

1878 Jul 29	Tom Hawkins D. 31r. 123m. Joe Fowler	London
1878 Aug 12	Tom Hawkins D. 51r. 205m. Joe Fowler	London
1880 Dec 5	Tommy Orange W. ret. 6 Jem Laxton (126-118)	London
1883 Jul 31	Jem Laxton W. 3 H. Solomons (122lb.)	London
	(Final of Championship Competition)	
1886 ?	Samuel Blakelock Won Tom Stirk (126lb.)	—
	(Final of Championship Competition)	
1886 —	Bill Baxter W. 12 Pudsey Sullivan (Belt)	Lambeth
1887 —	Bill Baxter won Jack Davis' Championship Comp. (126lb.)	
		St. Stephen's Hall
1888 —	Harry Mead W. 3 Stanton Abbott (126lb.)	—
	(Final of Championship Competition)	
1888 Mar 6	Bill Baxter W. 3 Stanton Abbott (126lb.)	Islington
	(Final of Championship Competition)	
1888 Apr 14	Fred Johnson W. 4 Pudsey Sullivan (122lb.)	London
	(Final of Championship Competition)	
1888 May 14	Billy Reader W. 10 Dave Burke (126lb.)	Haymarket
	(Final of Championship Competition)	
1888 Dec	Fred Johnson W. 4 Bill Baxter (122lb.)	London
	(Final of Championship Competition)	
1889 Mar	Harry Mead W. 6 Bill Baxter (126lb.)	London
	(Final of Championship Competition)	
1889 Mar 16	Fred Johnson W. 4 Bill Baxter (124lb.)	London
	(Final of Championship Competition)	
1889 Apr 25	Bill Baxter W. 4 Reuben Baxter (126lb.)	Wood Green
	(Final of Championship Competition)	
1889 ?	Bill Corbett W. 25 Harry Greenfield (122lb.)	—
1890 ?	Harry Spurden W. f. 39 Bill Corbett	Kennington
1890 Aug 22	Harry Overton W. ko 13 Billy Reader (126lb.)	Ormonde Club
1890 Sep 15	Harry Spurden W. 26 Bill Corbett	Lambeth
1890 Dec 5	Fred Johnson W. 4 Stanton Abbott (126lb.)	Kennington
	(Final of Championship Competition)	
1891 Apr 27	Billy Reader W. ko 16 Bill Baxter (126lb.)	N.S.C.
1891 Aug 15	Fred Johnson W. f. 10 James Howe (122lb.)	Walworth
1891 Nov 23	Billy Reader W. ko 4 Harry Overton	N.S.C.
1891 Dec 19	Stanton Abbott W. 4 Harry Spurden (126lb.)	Kennington
	(Final of Championship Competition)	
1892 Dec 19	Harry Spurden W. 20 Billy Reader (126lb.)	N.S.C.
1893 Apr 11	Morgan Crowther W. ko 20 Fred Johnson (124lb.)	London
1894 May 7	Fred Johnson W. ko 14 Dave Wallace (126lb.)	N.S.C.
1894 Jun 27	Harry Spurden W. 22 Darkey Barton (126lb.)	N.S.C.
1895 Feb 6	Jack Fitzpatrick W. ko 7 Harry Spurden (126lb.)	Clapham Junction
1895 Apr 22	George Johnson W. f. 2 Tom Causer (126lb.)	Holborn
	(Final of Championship Competition)	
1895 Apr 29	Fred Johnson W. ko 4 Charlie Beadling (120lb.)	Newcastle
1897 Jan 11	Harry Greenfield W. ko 13 Fred Johnson	London

1897 Feb 22	Ben Jordan W. ko 12 Fred Johnson (119lb.)	N.S.C.
1897 Mar 3	Harry Greenfield W. ko 8 Larry Barnes (126lb.)	Birmingham
1897 Nov 29	Ben Jordan W. ko 19 Tommy White (126lb.)	N.S.C.
1898 Feb 8	George Cunningham W. 6 Dick Tiddiman (126lb.) (Final of Championship Competition)	London
1898 Mar 7	Ted Marlow W. 10 Arthur Wilkinson (126lb.) (Final of Championship Competition)	Sheffield
1898 Mar 7	Tom Turner W. rsf 6 Harry Williams (120lb.) (Final of Championship Competition)	Sheffield
1898 Apr 4	Ben Jordan W. ret. 17 Eddie Curry (122lb.)	N.S.C.
1898 Apr 18	George Cunningham W. ko 3 Harry Spurden (126lb.) (Final of Championship Competition)	London
1899 May 29	Ben Jordan W. ko 9 Harry Greenfield (124lb.)	N.S.C.
1900 Jan 22	Will Curley W. 20 Nat Smith (122lb.)	Newcastle
1900 —	Jack Gibson Won Bob Russell (124lb.)	Newcastle
1901 Jan 21	Jack Roberts W. ko 7 Will Curley (126lb.)	N.S.C.
1901 Feb 16	Bert Adams Won Dick Lee (122lb.) (Final of Championship Competition)	Wonderland
1901 Apr 22	Jack Roberts W. ko 8 Billy Smith (126lb.)	N.S.C.
1902 Feb 3	Will Curley W. ko 3 Jack Roberts (126lb.)	Newcastle
1902 Feb 12	Bill Hough W. 6 Harry Chamberlain (126lb.) (Final of Championship Competition)	Wonderland
1902 May 28	Ben Jordan W. ko 4 Tommy Hogan	N.S.C.
1902 Oct 20	Ben Jordan W. ko 5 Jack Roberts (126lb.)	N.S.C.
1903 Dec 15	Will Curley W. ko 8 Pedler Palmer (124lb.)	Newcastle
1904 Jan 18	Wally Morgan W. 20 Charlie Lampey (122lb.)	London
1904 Apr 25	Alf Read W. 15 Jack Fitzpatrick (126lb.)	Haymarket
1904 Dec 12	Ben Jordan W. 15 Pedler Palmer (Jordan retired)	N.S.C.
1905 Mar 20	Joe Bowker W. rsf 12 Pedler Palmer (124lb.)	N.S.C.
1905 Oct 23	Joe Bowker W. 20 Spike Robson (122lb.)	N.S.C.
1906 Jan 29	Johnny Summers W. 20 Spike Robson (126lb.)	N.S.C.
1906 May 28	Jim Driscoll W. 15 Joe Bowker (123lb.)	N.S.C.
1906 Oct 1	Johnny Summers W. 20 Boss Edwards (124lb.)	N.S.C.
1906 Dec 17	Spike Robson W. f. 4 Johnny Summers	N.S.C.
1907 Mar 8	Harry Sterling Won Jimmy Hicks (Final of Championship Competition)	—
1907 Jun 1	Jim Driscoll W. ko 17 Joe Bowker (122lb.)	N.S.C.
1908 Feb 24	Jim Driscoll W. f. 15 Charlie Griffin (126lb.)	N.S.C.
1910 Feb 14	Jim Driscoll W. rsf 6 Arthur Hayes (Lonsdale Belt)	N.S.C.

BANTAMWEIGHT TITLE FIGHTS

| 1872 Apr 15 | George Dove W. 5 Jerry Hawkes (Bow Cup) (116lb.) (Final of Championship Competition) | Bow Grounds |

1877 Aug 8	George Dove W. ko 2 Jerry Hawkes	London
	(Dove retired)	
1878-1883	Jem Laxton Champion. (Presented with Championship Belt)	
1880s	Charlie Williams won Championship Competition. (114lb.)	
		London
1886 ?	Fred Johnson won over Dido Hopwood (118lb.)	Whitechapel
	(Final of Championship Competition)	
1888	Fred Johnson W. 3 Hippy Homer (118lb.)	Liverpool
	(Final of Championship Competition)	
1888 Dec 21	Bill Baxter W. ret. 42 Fred Johnson (118lb.)	London
1889 Feb 23	Arthur Wilkinson W. 4 Charles Mansford (114lb.)	London
	(Final of Championship Competition)	
1889 Mar 12	Nunc Wallace W. 9r. 40m. Bill Goode (112lb.)	London
1889 Mar 16	W. Holmes won Championship Competition (114lb.)	London
1889 Apr 25	Arthur Wesley W. 4 Charlie Smith (112lb.)	London
	(Final of Championship Competition)	
1890 ?	Tim Sullivan won over Bill Roberts (112lb.)	N.S.C.
	(Final of Championship Competition)	
1890 —	Charlie Smith won Championship Competition. (116lb.)	London
1890 —	Charlie Smith won Championship Competition. (116lb.)	London
1890 Jan 26	Bill Baxter W. 17 Morgan Crowther	Kennington
1891 Feb 13	Billy Plimmer W. ko 10 Charles Mansford	London
1891 May 30	Billy Plimmer W. ret. 15 Jem Stevens (112lb.)	N.S.C.
1892 Jan 28	Tom Gardner W. f. 11 Nunc Wallace (118lb.)	Kennington
1892 —	Bill Moore won over Bill Norton (112lb.)	—
	(Final of Championship Competition)	
1892 —	Willie Smith won over Tim Sullivan (114lb.)	Holborn
1892 Oct 5	Willie Smith W. 10 Tom Gardner (114lb.)	Kennington
1893 Jan 19	Nunc Wallace W. 24 Joe Portley (112lb.)	London
1895 Sep 9	George Corfield W. ko 18 Nunc Wallace (112lb.)	Sheffield
1895 Nov 25	Pedler Palmer W. f. 14 Billy Plimmer (112lb.)	N.S.C.
1896 Sep 7	Billy Plimmer W. 20 George Corfield (112lb.)	Sheffield
1897 Jan 25	Pedler Palmer W. rsf 14 Ernie Stanton (117lb.)	N.S.C.
1897 Jun —	Will Curley W. 20 Tom Turner (115lb.)	Gateshead
1897 Oct 18	Pedler Palmer W. 20 Dave Sullivan (116lb.)	N.S.C.
1898 Feb 25	Joe Barrett W. 12 Joe Elms (USA) (116lb.)	Birmingham
	(Final of Championship Competition)	
1898 Mar 8	George Corfield W. 10 Jack Walker (112lb.)	Sheffield
	(Final of Championship Competition)	
1898 Dec 12	Pedler Palmer W. rsf 17 Billy Plimmer	N.S.C.
1899 Feb 11	George Harding W. 6 Johnny Thomas (118lb.)	Wonderland
	(Final of Championship Belt Competition)	
1900 Feb 12	Harry Ware W. 20 Billy Plimmer (114lb.)	Manchester
1900 Apr 6	Patsy Walsh W. 6 Jim Williams (118lb.)	Wonderland
	(Final of Championship Competition)	

E

1900 May 28	Pedler Palmer W. 15 Harry Ware (114lb.)	N.S.C.
1900 Nov 12	Harry Ware W. 20 Pedler Palmer (114lb.)	N.S.C.
1901 Jan 6	Bill Stonelake W. ko 3 Dick Parkes (116lb.)	Wonderland
	(Final of Championship Competition)	
1901 Feb 13	Andrew Tokell W. ko 4 George Corfield (114lb.)	Newcastle
1902 Jan 27	Jim Williams W. ko 2 Pedler Palmer (116lb.)	N.S.C.
1902 Feb 3	Cockney Cohen W. ko 10 Johnny Thomas (117lb.)	Leeds
1902 Feb 13	Andrew Tokell W. 20 Harry Ware (114lb.)	London
1902 May 12	Andrew Tokell W. f. 10 Jim Williams (114lb.)	N.S.C.
1902 Jun	Johnny Hughes won Coronation Championship Belt.	N.S.C.
1902 Jun 26	Bill Stonelake W. 4 Alf Payne (118lb.)	Strand
	(Coronation Championship Belt)	
1902 Dec 15	Joe Bowker W. 15 Harry Ware	N.S.C.
1903 May 25	Joe Bowker W. 15 Andrew Tokell (116lb.)	N.S.C.
1903 Oct 3	Joe Bowker W. 15 Bill King (116lb.)	N.S.C.
1903 Nov 9	Joe Bowker W. rsf 9 Alf Fellowes (116lb.)	N.S.C.
1904 May 30	Joe Bowker W. 20 Owen Moran (116lb.)	N.S.C.
1905 Jan 23	Owen Moran W. 20 Digger Stanley (114lb.)	N.S.C.
1905 May 29	Joe Bowker W. 20 Pinky Evans (116lb.)	London
	(Bowker fought in Featherweight Division)	
1905 Nov 2	Owen Moran W. ko 3 Alf Fellowes	Liverpool
1906 Dec 13	Digger Stanley W. 20 Ike Bradley (114lb.)	Liverpool
1907 Apr 22	Owen Moran W. 20 Al Delmont	N.S.C.
	(Moran outgrew division)	
1908 Mar 20	Digger Stanley W. 15 Ike Bradley	London
1908 Oct 19	Digger Stanley W. 20 Sam Kellar	London
1910 Oct 17	Digger Stanley W. ko 8 Joe Bowker (Lonsdale Belt)	N.S.C.

FLYWEIGHT & PAPERWEIGHT TITLE FIGHTS

1885 ?	Jem Stevens W. 6 Art Levy (84lb.)	—
1888 Feb 23	Patsy Sheehan W. 4 Billy Plimmer (104lb.)	London
1889 Oct	Jim Pope D. 24r. 96m. Alf Gunning (104lb.)	London
1890 ?	Alf Gower Won Patsy Sheehan (106lb.)	—
	(Final of Championship Competition)	
1890 Aug 11	Billy Plimmer W. ko 13 Arthur Wesley (110lb.)	London
1890 Dec	Jem Stevens W. 5 Tommy De Groat (102lb.)	London
1891 —	Bill Mortimore W. 8 Joe Gates (96lb.)	—
1891 ?	Alf Gower Won George Little (106lb.)	—
	(Final of Championship Competition)	
1892 ?	Mike Small W. 5 Bill Mortimore (102lb.)	—
1892 Feb 1	Joe Bennett W. 15 Mike Lanigan (90lb.)	London
1892 Feb 16	Bill Bolton W. f. 8 Alf Buckingham (102lb.)	Bermondsey
1892 ?	Alf Gower W. 4 Arthur Wesley (106lb.)	Goodwin Club
1892 Sep 19	Joe Bennett W. 11 Walter Croot (92lb.)	Kennington

1892 Oct 24	Bill Mortimore W. 15 Bill Bolton (Belt) (102lb.)	N.S.C.
1893 Mar 13	George Beach W. ko 20 Bill Mortimore (102lb.)	N.S.C.
1893 May 1	Pedler Palmer W. ko 17 Walter Croot (100lb.)	N.S.C.
1893 Oct 10	Mike Small W. 3 Harry Brown (102lb.)	Wolverhampton
1893 Oct 31	Jack Maloney W. 9 Harry Munroe (94lb.)	London
1893 Dec 11	George Corfield W. 20 Chappie Moran (110lb.)	Sheffield
1894 Feb 1	Jack Maloney W. 6 Harry Munroe (92lb.)	London
1894 Mar 9	Jack Maloney W. ko 12 Joe Bennett (94lb.)	London
1894 May 21	George Corfield W. 20 Bill Moore (110lb.)	Sheffield
1894 Jun 25	Pedler Palmer W. 5 Bill Mortimore (104lb.)	N.S.C.
1894 Jul 30	Chappie Moran W. 20 Jack Fitzpatrick (107lb.)	Sheffield
1894 Sep 10	George Corfield W. ret. 12 Alf Gower (110lb.)	Sheffield
1894 Dec 3	Mike Small W. rsf 18 Ernest Pickard (102lb.)	N.S.C.
1895 Feb 12	Albert Gould W. f. 1 Jim Williams (104lb.)	Kilburn
1895 Feb 25	Jack Pearson W. 20 Mike Small (102lb.)	N.S.C.
1895 Mar	Jim Williams Won Dick Parkes (106lb.)	Holborn
	(Final of Championship Competition)	
1895 ?	Tim Buckley W. 19r. 85m. Sid Phillips (104lb.)	—
1895 May 28	Billy Plimmer W. ko 7 George Corfield (110lb.)	N.S.C.
1895 Jun 3	Jack Maloney W. 20 Charlie Gledhill (94lb.)	Newcastle
1896 Jan 28	Ted Beach W. f. 12 Jack Maloney (98lb.)	Kennington
1896 Mar 30	Harry McDermott W. 20 Jack Maloney (98lb.)	Jarrow-on-Tyne
1896 —	George Bishop won Championship Competition. (98lb.)	
		Abe Hicken's
1896 Oct	Jack Pearson W. 20 Mike Small (102lb.)	N.S.C.
1896 Oct 19	Harry McDermott W. 15 Ted Beach (104lb.)	Gateshead
1896 —	Harry McDermott W. ko 4 James Freeman (106lb.)	Holloway
1896 Nov 30	Walter Croot W. 11 Mike Small (102lb.)	N.S.C.
1897 Jan 4	Ike Cohen W. rsf 9 Joe Gates (102lb.)	N.S.C.
1897 Feb 8	Ted Beach W. 20 Harry Brodigan (98lb.)	Gateshead
1897 Feb 8	Bob Bailey W. 20 Ike Cohen (104lb)	Sheffield
1897 Apr 26	Jack Pearson D. 20 Peter McDermott (100lb.)	Dublin
1897 Jul 6	Joe Williams W. ko 16 Mike Kerwin (91lb.)	Birmingham
1897 Aug 2	Mike Small W. ko 7 Bob Bailey (104lb.)	Walworth
1897 Nov 1	Jack Walker W. rsf 3 Johnny Thomas (108lb.)	N.S.C.
1897 Nov 18	Joe Williams W. ko 4 Curley Wood (94lb.)	London
1897 Nov 22	Harry McDermott W. ko 17 Ernest Brady (104lb.)	Gateshead
1898 ?	Harry Slough W. 1 Harry McDermott (104lb.)	—
1898 ?	Jack Guyon won Championship Belt. (108lb.)	Wonderland
1898 Feb 25	Harry McDermott W. rsf 7 Charlie Taylor (104lb.)	Sheffield
1898 Mar 1	George Beach W. ko 5 Harry McDermott (104lb.)	Sheffield
1898 Mar 5	George Beach W. 10 Matt Precious (104lb.)	Sheffield
	(Final of Championship Competition)	
1898 Mar 14	Ted Beach W. 20 Joe Williams	N.S.C.
1898 Apr 4	Charlie Exall W. f. 17 Harry Brodigan (104lb.)	Gateshead

1898 —	Jim Williams Won George Murray (84lb.)	Leeds
	(Final of Championship Competition)	
1898 —	Jim Williams Won Ted Beach (94lb.)	—
1898 ?	Charlie Exall W. 20 Jack Walker (108lb.)	London
1898 Aug ?	Ted Beach won Champions Cup (98lb.)	—
1898 Nov 28	Mike Riley W. 20 Charlie Exall (104lb.)	N.S.C.
1899 Feb 20	Dave Job W. rsf 14 Jack Guyon (104lb.)	N.S.C.
1899 Apr 1	Harry McDermott W. ko 14 Charlie Exall (102lb.)	Gateshead
	(Exall 3lb. overweight)	
1899 May 29	Charlie Exall W. rsf 19 Mike Riley (104lb)	Gateshead
1900 Jan 20	Matt Precious W. ko 9 Mike Riley (106lb.)	N.S.C.
1900 Feb 12	Dave Job W. ko 12 Ted Beach (102lb.)	N.S.C.
1900 Apr 20	Harry McDermott W. rsf 8 Kid Veitch (108lb.)	Newcastle
1900 —	Jim Kenrick W. ko 14 Kid Veitch (108lb.)	Gateshead
1901 Nov 4	Charlie Exhall W. ko 6 Matt Precious (104lb.)	Newcastle
1901 Jun 17	Digger Stanley W. 20 Owen Moran (100lb.)	Birmingham
1901 Jul 22	Harry McDermott W. 20 Charlie Exall (108lb.)	Gateshead
1901 Dec 22	Jack Walker W. 15 Ernest Moody (110lb.)	London
1902 Feb 10	Charlie Exall W. 20 Jack Walker (106lb.)	London
1902 Feb	Mike Riley W. ret. 10 Matt Precious (106lb.)	N.S.C.
1902 Apr 21	Jim Kendrick W. 15 Dave Job (112lb.)	N.S.C.
1902 May 12	Owen Moran W. 10 Jim Kenrick (110lb.)	N.S.C.
1902 Nov 15	Harry McDermott W. 15 Jim Kenrick	Newcastle
1902 Dec ?	Charlie Exall W. ko 8 Harry McDermott (106lb.)	Newcastle
1903 Jan 17	Charlie Exall D. 15 Jim Kenrick (106lb.)	Newcastle
1903 Jan 24	Dave Job W. ko 4 Harry McDermott (107lb.)	Newcastle
1903 Feb 14	Eddie Sullivan W. rsf 7 Barney Sloan (94lb.)	Newcastle
1903 Feb 23	Jim Kenrick W. 20 Charlie Exall (106lb.)	Newcastle
1903 Mar 2	Digger Stanley W. 12 Jack Walker (110lb.)	London
1903 May 25	Owen Moran W. 15 Jack Walker (112lb.)	N.S.C.
1903 Nov 9	Digger Stanley W. 15 Owen Moran (112lb.)	N.S.C.
1903 Dec 14	Digger Stanley W. 15 Jack Walker (112lb.)	N.S.C.
1904 Jun 20	Owen Moran W. 10 Jack Fitzpatrick (112lb.)	Barking
1904 Jun 30	Jack Wise W. 15 Frank Morecambe (106lb.)	Canning Town
1904 Aug 1	Boyo Driscoll W. 10 Owen Moran (112lb.)	Cardiff
1905 Feb 27	Jim Kenrick W. 15 Boyo Driscoll (112lb.)	N.S.C.
1905 Aug 24	Owen Moran W. ko 7 Jim Kenrick (105lb.)	Liverpool
1909 Sep 29	Joey Smith W. 20 Eddie Morgan (106lb.)	Pontypridd
1910 Jan 31	Harry McDermott W. 20 Joe Percival (105lb.)	Newcastle
1910 Apr 7	Albert Cocksedge W. 20 Harry McDermott (105lb.)	Newcastle
1911 Sep 25	Sid Smith W. 20 Bill Hoskyne	'The Ring'
1911 Oct 19	Sid Smith W. 20 Louis Ruddick (112lb.)	Liverpool
1911 Dec 4	Sid Smith W. 20 Joe Wilson (Lonsdale Belt) (112lb.)	N.S.C.
1912 Sep 19	Sid Smith W. 20 Curley Walker	'The Ring'
1913 Jan 1	Jimmy Wilde W. ret. 18 Billy Paddon (98lb.)	Glasgow

STANTON ABBOTT

Born 23rd June, 1867. London

	1887	
	Jack Kibble W. 6	Willesden
	Harry Williams W. 6	Epsom
	Fred Mansfield W. 6	Dartmouth
	Tommy Walker W. 9	Kennington
	Harry Osborne L. 12	London
	Ginger Elmer W. 12	Lambeth
Dec	Bill Donoghue W. 3	Blackfriars
	1888	
	Tommy Walker Won	Islington
	Harry Mead Won	Islington
	Bill Gibbs Won	Islington
	Bill Hook Won	Islington
Mar 6	Bill Baxter L. 3	Islington

(Final of 126lb. Championship Competition)

	Ginger Elmer W. 12	N.S.C.
	Harry Mead L. 3	—

(Final of 126lb. Championship Competition)

Jul 6	Dick Gannon W. 3	London
Jul 26	George Johnson W. 3	—
Oct 5	M. Hyams L. 4	—
Nov 12	Jem Crimmons W. ko 5	—
Dec 5	Harry Denny L. 3	—
Dec 11	George Wilson L. 3	—
	1889	
Jan 4	Harry Osborne L. 12	—
Feb 20	Harry Mead L. 3	—
Feb 23	Billy Reader Won	—
Aug 13	Billy Willis W. ko 12	—
Dec 9	Harry Denny L. 3	—
	1890	
—	Ted Willis W. 9	London
—	Tom Biscon W. 6	Kennington
Dec 4	Fred Johnson L. 4	Kennington

(English Nine Stone Title)

Dec 15	J. Edwin L. ko 6	London
	1891	
Mar 17	Ginger Elmer W. 12	—
Oct 5	Bill Baxter W. ko 12	N.S.C.

1892

Feb 29	Harry Overton W. 12	N.S.C.
Oct 10	Sam Baxter L. 10	N.S.C.
Dec 19	Harry Spurden W. 4	Kennington

(Final of 126lb. Championship Competition)

1893

Jan 23	Sam Baxter W. ret. 18	N.S.C.
—	Owen Ziegler D. 4	—
Apr 29	Jack Hopper W. 2	New York

1894

Jan 8	Jack Falvey W. ret. 15	Providence
Feb 28	Harry Gilmore W. ko 5	Chicago
Mar 26	Willie Clark W. ko 3	New York
Mar 27	Billy Dacey W. ko 1	New York
Apr 7	Bull McCarthy D. 6	New York
May 7	Andy Bowen D. 10	New Orleans
Jul 4	Billy Myer W. 15	Boston
Jul 19	Johnny Young W. ko 9	Alexandria
Aug 21	Jack Everhardt L. ko 25	New Orleans
Sep 25	Jack Everhardt D. 25	New Orleans
Oct 13	Owen Ziegler L. 13	Philadelphia
Oct 30	Charlie Gehring W. ko 3	Baltimore
Dec 5	Jack Hanley L. 4	Philadelphia
Dec 20	Charlie McKeever L. 6	Philadelphia

1895

Feb 27	Tom Hayes W. 8	New York
Feb 28	George Mickle W. 6	New Bedford
Mar 14	Charlie Gehring ND 6	Baltimore
Mar 17	Owen Ziegler L. 9	Philadelphia
Mar 19	Owen Ziegler ND 6	Philadelphia
May 1	Jack Falway D. 6	Providence
May 15	Al O'Brien W. 6	New York
Jun 3	Leslie Pierce L. 20	Boston
Jun 14	Jack Burke D. 15	Montreal
Jul 8	Billy Dyke W. ko 8	Eureka
Aug 19	Owen Ziegler L. 20	Eureka
Dec 30	Jack Daly D. 37	Eureka

1896

Jan 13	Al O'Brien D. 6	South Bethlehem
Feb 14	Leslie Pierce D. 15	Boston
Feb 26	Tom Moriaty D. 20	Holyoke
Mar 2	Paddy Sheehan D. 6	South Bethlehem
Apr 20	Paddy Fenton D. 8	Boston
Jul 4	Johnny Young D. 10	Albany
Oct 29	Matty Matthews L. ko 7	New York

Dec 5	Mike Leonard L. ko 3	Brooklyn
—	Kid McPartland L. 3	New York
	1897	
Jan 18	Jack Bennett L. 6	Philadelphia
Mar 9	Dan McConnell L. 12	Trenton
Mar 29	Mike Fanagher L. 7	New York
Sep 6	Jack Falvey L. 15	Newport
Oct 25	Maurice Hagerstone W. 9	Long Isle
Nov 24	Leslie Pierce ND 4	Philadelphia
Nov 29	Joe Gans L. 5	Baltimore
Dec 7	Jack Randall ND 4	Philadelphia
Dec 16	Billy Ernst D. 6	Paterson

TOM ALLEN

Born April, 1840.   Birmingham, England.   Died 5th April, 1904.

	1861	
Mar 21	Morris Connor W. 12r. 42m. (£20)	Nr. Birmingham
Nov 21	Jack Gould W. 25r. 65m. (136-) (£30)	Birmingham District
—	Waggoner L. 30m.	—
	1862	
Apr 20	Jem White Won (£10)	—
Jul 28	Posh Price L. 35r. 50m. (£20)	Sutton Coldfield
	1864	
Jan 28	Bingley Rose W. 10r. 22m. (140lb.) (£100)	Home Circuit
Jun 2	Bob Smith L. 50r. 135m. (£10)	Hilbury Island
(English Welterweight Championship)		
	1865	
Jun 13	Jack Parkinson W. 11r. 23m. (152lb.) (£50)	Four Ashes
Nov 28	Posh Price W. 41r. 125m. (£50)	Holly Lane, Staffs.
	1866	
Jun 13	George Iles W. 17r. 62m. (157-176) (£50)	Kingswood Common
	1867	
Mar 5	Joe Goss D. 31r. 102m. (157-164) (£200)	Nr. St. Malins
(English Middleweight Championship)		
July 21	Went to America	
	1869	
Jan 12	Bill Davis W. 43r. ($2,000)	Chatteau Isle
(American Heavyweight Championship)		
Feb 23	Charlie Gallagher L. 2r. 3m. ($4,000)	Carroll Isle
(American Heavyweight Championship)		
Jun 15	Mike McCoole L. f. 9r. (182-196) ($2,000)	Foster Isle
(American Heavyweight Championship)		

Aug 17 Charlie Gallagher 11r. 25m. (Dispute) ($2,000)   Foster Isle
(American Heavyweight Championship)
> *1870*

May 10 Jem Mace L. 10r. 44m. (173-168) ($5,000)   Kennerville
(World Heavyweight Championship)

Oct 8 Charlie Gallagher W. 16r. 23½m. ($1,000)   St. Louis
> *1873*

Sep 23 Mike McCoole W. 7r. 20m. ($500)   Chatteau Isle
(World Heavyweight Championship)

Nov 18 Ben Hogan W. 3r. (Riot)   Council Buffs
(World Heavyweight Championship)
> *1876*

— Jem Mace L. Pts.   —

Sept 7 Joe Goss L. f. 21r. 112m. (Two rings) ($5,000)
(American Heavyweight Championship)   Kenton & Boon Counties
> *1877*

Oct 29 Tomkin Gilbert W. Ret. 7r. 16m. 25s. (Gloves) (£200)
(English Heavyweight Championship)   Sadlers Wells
> *1878*

Apr 4 Charley Davis W. Disq. 5r. 18m. 25s. (Gloves) (£200)
(English Heavyweight Championship)   Cambridge Heath
> *1879*

Apr 22 Jem Stewart D. 25r. 100m. (189-170) (£200)   St. James Hall
(English Heavyweight Championship)
> *1882*

Nov 27 George Rooke Exh. 3r.   New York
> *1884*

Jan 7 Fidler Neary Exh.   New York

CHARLIE ALLUM

Born 23rd April, 1876.   (Nephew of Ben Caunt)   Died July, 1918.

— Ted Francis W. rsf 2   N.S.C.
> *1903*

Apr 6 Fred Blackwell W. ko 2   N.S.C.

Apr 18 Peter Brown L. 6   London

Sep 12 Charlie Knock L. 6   London

Nov 16 Charlie Knock W. ko 9   London
(English Welterweight Title)
> *1904*

Feb 1 Charlie Knock L. 12   London
(English Welterweight Title)

Apr 18	Pat O'Keefe W. 6	London
Jun 4	Jack Clancy L. ko 3	Newcastle
(English 10st. 6lb. Title)		
Nov 21	Young Peter Jackson L. ko 6	London
	1905	
Feb 27	Jack Kingsland W. ko 10	N.S.C.
(Claimed Middleweight Title)		
Jun 29	Harry Smith W. ko 5	Liverpool
Nov 24	Willie Burke W. ko 3	Paris
Dec 18	Pat O'Keefe D. 6	N.S.C.
	1906	
Feb 23	Bill Higgins W. 10	Paris
Apr 23	Pat O'Keefe L. ko 6	N.S.C.
Sep 8	Frank Craig L. ko 5	London
	1907	
Mar 2	Pat O'Keefe L. 7	Paris
Aug 31	Mike Crawley W. 2	London
Sep 14	Pat O'Keefe L. pts. 6	London
Oct 5	Jack Scales L. 6	London
Nov 14	Tiger Smith L. 1	Merthyr
	1908	
Apr 11	Jack Costello L. 6	London
Apr 27	Jewey Smith L. 2	London
Aug 15	Jack Williams W. 6	London
	1909	
Jan 25	Joe Smith W. 8	London
Mar 29	Jack Kingsland D. 20	Putney
Jul 3	Jim Sullivan L. 6	London
Oct 4	Ted Nelson L. 15	N.S.C.
	1910	
Sept 12	Frank Inglis W. 6	London
	Undated Contest	
	Harry Shearing D. 6	—

JOE BARRETT

Born 10th August, 1878. (Joseph Richard Burrett) Bermondsey.
Died 27th December, 1953.

	1894	
Dec 15	Jack Guyon L. 8	Lambeth
	1895	
Jan 13	Sam Knowles L. 1	Bermondsey
Feb 18	Bob Mead W. 8	Bermondsey

Mar 2	Mike Singleton Won	Bermondsey
Mar 9	Jack Guyon L. 6	Bermondsey
Mar 18	Joe Johnson Lost	Bermondsey
Apr 7	Harry Gebbitt W. 4	Bermondsey
Jul 29	Bill Nixon W. 6	Bermondsey
Oct 12	Bill Small Won	Bermondsey
Oct 19	Dick Davenport W. 4	Bermondsey
Nov 23	Patsy Walsh Won	Bermondsey
Dec 2	Wall Smith Won	Bermondsey
Dec 16	Patsy Walsh L. 6	Bermondsey
	1896	
Jan 19	Wall Smith W. 6	Bermondsey
Jan 20	Wall Smith W. 6	Bermondsey
Feb 6	Wall Smith W. 9	Westminster
Mar 2	Taff Davies W. 3	Amberley
Mar 2	G. Harrison W. ko 1	Amberley
Mar 2	Jem Preston W. ko 2	Amberley
Apr 8	Jack Walker L. ko 12	Amberley
Aug 29	Joe Parker W. 6	Shoreditch
Sep 26	Bill Hoad L. 6	Shoreditch
Sep 30	George Munroe W. 4	Tom Symond's
Oct 8	George Gladding L. 12	Queensbury C.C.
	1897	
Feb 10	George Gladding L. 6	Bethnal Green
Feb 15	Bill Fielder W. 6	Shoreditch
Feb 18	George Gladding W. 6	Bethnal Green
Feb 20	Charlie Broadbank Lost	Holloway
Mar 8	George Gladding L. 8	Wonderland
Apr 26	Charlie Broadbank L. 8	Pentonville
May 8	Jack Moore L. 6	Newmarket
Sep 11	Charlie Broadbank W. 6	Glengall Gym.
Sep 20	Dan Cripps W. 8	Glengall Gym.
Sep 27	Bill Richardson W. 8	Glengall Gym.
Sep 29	Bill Hullett W. 6	Newmarket
Oct 14	Bill Hullett W. 6	Newmarket
Oct 30	Jack Jones W. 6	Glengall Gym.
Nov 2	Bill Richardson W. 8	Tottenham
Nov 9	Bill Percy W. 6	Pentonville
Nov 20	Sid Scales L. 6	Bethnal Green
Nov 25	Bill Hoad W. 8	West End S.A.
Nov 25	George Gladding W. 6	Bethnal Green
Dec 6	Bill Hoad W. 6	Tottenham
Dec 13	Dan Dudley W. 6	Tottenham
Dec 16	Harry Newman W. 6	Glengall Gym.
Dec 18	Sid Scales W. 6	Woolwich

Dec 31	George Slark W. 10	Bethnal Green
	1898	
Jan 24	Sid Scales L. 10	N.S.C.
Jan 31	George Slark W. 10	Bethnal Green
Feb 6	Fred Delaney L. 6	N.S.C.
Feb 10	Bill Hoad W. 6	Bethnal Green
Feb 12	Bill Butler W. 6	Woolwich
Feb 18	Joe Whinney W. 5	Birmingham
Feb 23	Jack Moore W. 10	Birmingham
Feb 25	Joe Elms W. 12 (USA)	Birmingham
(Final of 8st. 4lb. Championship Competition)		
Mar 6	Andrew Wood	Gateshead
Mar —	Jack Walker Lost	Sheffield
Apr 14	Dick Tarr W. 6	Newmarket
Oct 20	Wag Lansdowne W. 10	Newmarket
Nov 10	Bill Fielder W. 6	Hackney
Nov 21	Bill Pike W. 6	Bayswater
Nov 30	Bill Richardson D. 20	Paris
Dec 3	Wag Lansdowne W. 6	Woolwich
Dec 5	Fred Homewood W. 6	Bayswater
Dec 11	Bill Hullett W. 6	Hackney
Dec 13	Fred Herring W. 6	Soho
Dec 23	Bill Richardson W. 10	Woolwich
Dec 28	Ted Goodson W. 6	Northampton
	1899	
Jan 9	George Slark W. 10	Bayswater
Jan 30	Fred Herring L. 10	Bayswater
Feb 7	Arthur Abbott W. 10	Wonderland
Feb 8	George Harding L. 10	Wonderland
Feb 20	Dick Ashton W. 6	N.S.C.
May 8	Bill Richardson L. ko 9	N.S.C.
—	Jack Hennessy nd 3	—
Jul 12	Bill Hullett W. 10	Newmarket
Aug 28	Bill Hullett W. 10	Glengall Gym.
Nov 30	Toby McKenzie W. 8	Woolwich
	1900	
Feb 25	Bill Hutchinson W. 3	Goodwin Club
Feb 25	Bill Maher W. ret. 2	Goodwin Club
Feb 25	Fred Delaney W. ret. 2	Goodwin Club
Mar 23	Johnny Thomas L. ko 13	N.S.C.
—	Harry Churchill L. 8	—
—	George Proctor L. 4	Wonderland
—	Bill Fielder L. 6	—
	1902	
Jan 24	Boss Edwards L. 6	N.S.C.

BILL BAXTER

Born 16th October, 1860.

1881		
Won Punch Lewis Cup Competition		Spitalfields
Won Lightweight Cup Competition		Chelsea
Won Jack Ewan's £10 Competition		Brick Lane
Won Cup Competition		Shoreditch
1881-1885		
—	Fred Johnson Lost	Snaresbrook
—	Bill Hook Lost	Shoreditch
(Final of Lightweight Competition)		
Won Bob Habbijam's 8st. 6lb. Champion Belt		
—	Dave Burke Lost	Westminster
(Final of 8st. Competition)		
1886		
—	Pudsey Sullivan W. 12	Lambeth
(Harry Clarke's Champion Belt)		
—	Owen Hannan W. 6	Shoreditch
1887		
Won Jack Davis' 9st. Champion Belt		St. Stephen's Hall
—	Harry Mead Won	—
—	Harry Mead Lost	Westminster
1888		
—	Tommy Walker W. 12	—
—	Mark Dooley W. 8	—
—	Evan Davies Won	—
Mar 6	Stanton Abbott W. 3	Islington
(Final of 9st. Championship Competition)		
Apr 10	Fred Fox W. 4	London
Dec —	Fred Johnson L. 4	London
(Final of Ben Hyam's 8st. 10lb. Competition)		
Dec 21	Fred Johnson W. ret. 42	Kennington
(English Bantamweight Title)		
1889		
Feb 23	Fred Johnson L. 4	London
(Final of 8st. 8lb. Championship Competition)		
Mar 1	— Greenfield W. ret. 1	London
Mar —	— Farron Won	London
Mar —	Harry Mead L. 6	St. Stephen's Hall
(Final of 9st. Championship Competition)		
Mar 16	Fred Johnson L. 4	London
(Final of 8st. 12lb. Championship Competition)		

Apr 25	Billy Reader W. 3	Wood Green
Apr 27	Sam Baxter W. 4	Wood Green
(Final of 9st. Championship Competition)		
—	Harry Mead W. 6	Pentonville
—	Fred Johnson L. 3	London
	1890	
Jan 26	Morgan Crowther W. 17	Kennington
Mar 31	Fred Johnson W. dis. 6	Pelican Club
Apr 7	Fred Johnson L. 20	Pelican Club
	1891	
—	Ginger Elmer L. 4	Kennington
Apr 27	Billy Reader L. ko 16	N.S.C.
(English Featherweight Title)		
Oct 5	Stanton Abbott L. ko 12	N.S.C.
	1894	
Mar 2	Fred Johnson L. 6	Kennington
—	Charley Williams Won	London
	1897	
May 17	Harry Mead W. 6	N.S.C.

SAMUEL BLAKELOCK

Born 10th June, 1863.

Commenced Boxing in 1880 and won thirty-two consecutive competitions.

	Bill Gee W. 7	
	Tom Stirk W. (20gn. Cup)	Long Acre
(Final of 9st. Championship Competition)		
	Ben Seth W.	West End SoA.
	Evan Davies W.	West End SoA.
	Reuben Baxter W.	
	Harry Miller W.	
	Bill Murphy W.	
	'Deaf' Boon W.	
	Dido Hopwood W.	
	Joe Gates W.	
	Harry Cummings W.	
	Dan Cran W.	
	Harry Rumble W.	
	Bill Roberts W.	
	Harry Ewans W.	
	Shadow Anderson W.	
	Brother Ryan W.	

	Jim Hagen W.	
	Harry Keef W.	
	Albert Dixon W.	
	Harry Mathan W.	
	Mickey Moore W.	
	George Spooner W.	
	Jim Hooper W.	
	Tommy Mallett W.	
	Reuben Baxter W.	Lambeth
	Reuben Baxter W.	Lambeth
	Evan Davies W.	
	Jim Laxton D. 6	
	Dido Hopwood W. 6	
	Dido Hopwood D. 12	
	Tom Stirk W. 12	
	Albert Dixon W. 6	
	Billy Reader W.	
	1888	
	Tom Euston W.	Brighton
	Tom Euston W. 7m. (Knuckles)	—
	1889	
Mar 19	Jimmy Carroll L. ko 16	San Francisco
(World Lightweight Title)		
Oct 14	Billy Reader L. 12	London
	1890	
Mar 11	Dave Burke W. dis. 7	Kennington
	1891	
Jan 26	Jem Verrall L. ko 17	Walworth
	1892	
Mar 24	Reuben Baxter W. 15	Manchester

BILL BROOKS

Born 1849.   Mile End.   (William Biggs)

Died in training December 11th, 1872.

	1872	
Apr 2	— McGeehan W. 3	Soho
Apr 15	Jem Stewart W. 5 (Bow Cup)	Bow Grounds
(Final of Eleven Stone Championship Competition)		
Dec 1	Forfeited £10 to Albert Austin (Illness)	

DICK BURGE

Born 19th December, 1865.   Cheltenham.   Died 14th April, 1918.

	1882	
—	Reuben Smith W. 22m.	Birmingham
	1884	
—	Bob Foster W. 21m.	Newcastle
—	Jim Lowe W. 22m.	Newcastle
—	Jim Lowe W. 12m.	Newcastle
	1887	
Feb 14	Ben Seth L. pts. 8	London
May 4	Felix Scott W. ret. 5	Liverpool
Oct —	Frank Howson W. 8	Manchester
	1888	
Apr 23	Frank Howson L. f. 2	Sheffield
Nov 5	Johnny Robinson D. 12	Newcastle
(English 9st. 12lb. Title)		
	1889	
Jan 21	Anthony Diamond L. 12	Newcastle
Mar 5	Bill Goode Exh. 3	London
	1891	
May 25	Jem Carney W. f. 11	London
(World & English Lightweight Titles) (Two Ounce skin gloves)		
	1892	
Jun 27	Lachie Thompson W. ko 2	London
(English Welterweight Title) (144-138)		
Nov —	Austin Gibbons Exh. 4	Leeds
	1894	
Mar 1	Bill Hatcher Exh.	Leeds
Mar 2	Bill Hatcher Exh.	Leeds
Mar 3	Joe Wilson Exh.	Leeds
May 4	Harry Nickless W. ko 28	London
(English Ten Stone Title)		
Nov 26	Ted Pritchard L. ko 2	London
(English Middleweight Title)		
	1895	
Jan 21	Tom Williams W. ko 4	N.S.C.
(English Welterweight Title)		
Oct 14	Jem Mace Exh. 3	N.S.C.
Nov 26	Jem Smith L. dis. 9	Clapham Junction
(English Heavyweight Title)		

1896
Jun 1   George Lavigne L. rsf. 17   N.S.C.
(World Lightweight Title) (138lb.)
1897
Jan 28   Eddie Connolly D. 10   Birmingham
(English Welterweight Title) (146lb.)
May 31   Tom Causer L. f. 7   N.S.C.
(English Welterweight Title) (142-133)
Oct 8   Tom Causer W. ko 1   London
(English Welterweight Title)
Dec 31   Dick O'Brien W. f. 4   Birmingham
(English Middleweight Title)
1898
Sep 5   Arthur Akers W. ko 1   London
(English Middleweight Title)
Dec 12   Bobby Dobbs L. dis. 8   London
(World 10st. 4lb. Title)
1900
Jan —   Jerry Driscoll n/c   Gateshead
Feb 9   Jack Scales W. ko 1   London
(English Middleweight Title)
1910
May 14   Young Joseph Exh. 3   London
1914
Jan 15   Jack McAuliffe Exh. 3   London

TOM CAUSER

Born 15th January, 1872.   Bermondsey.

Amateur Bouts
George Costin W. 6
George Smith Won
1891-1893
Jem Egden W.
Patsy Travers W.   Bermondsey
Bert Smith W. 2   Croydon
George Bulton W. 6
Alf Watson W. 5
Jack Medge D.
Charles Fordham W. 4
G. Spillie W.
Sam Newman W.
Bill Lloyd W.   Lambeth
Alf Levy W. 6

Ted Vaughan W. 4
Jem Milton W. 3
Tom Reed W.
Tom Ashwick W. 3
Albert Young W. 20
Bill Theobald W.   Lambeth
George Costin W.
Albert Young W.
Tom Norton W.
Nov 27   Ted Gamble W. 16   Raglan Music Hall
          1894
Apr 16   Charles Tilley W.   London
Apr 16   Tom Tilley W.   London
Apr 16   Jack Loader W. 3   London
(Final of Frank Inde's 9st. 2lb. Competition)
Apr —   Tom Ireland W. 11   N.S.C.
Oct 6   Harry Greenfield W. 11   London
Nov 26   Tom Ashwick W. ko 2   Holborn
(English Lightweight Title)
          1895
Apr 22   George Johnson L. f. 2   Holborn
(Final of English 9st. Championship Competition)
          1896
Nov 22   Eddie Connolly L. ko 5   Birmingham
(World 9st. 6lb. Title)
Dec —   Walter Eyles W. 4   Birmingham
Dec —   Tom Ireland W. 6   Birmingham
Dec 29   Maurice Greenfield W. ret. 5   Birmingham
(Final of 9st. 8lb. Championship Competition)
          1897
May 27   Dick Burge W. f. 7 (133-142)   N.S.C.
(English Welterweight Title) (144lb.)
Oct 8   Dick Burge L. ko 1   London
(English Welterweight Title)
          1898
Mar 6   Arthur Lock W. 10   Sheffield
(Final of 9st. 8lb. Championship Competition)
—   Jewey Cooke D. 4   —

GEORGE CHRISP

Born 23rd February, 1872.   Newcastle-upon-Tyne.

John Brady W. ko 1   Sunderland

F

	1890	
Dec 18	George Cooper W. 8	Hull
	1891	
	James Lowe W. 9	Newcastle
	1892	
Jan 30	Harry Downie W. 4 (£80)	Newcastle
	1893	
Mar 6	Ted White L. 3	N.S.C.
Apr 24	Ted White L. 20 (154lb.)	N.S.C.
(English Middleweight Title)		
	1893-1894	
	Victor Layton W.	
	Jack Thompson W.	
	Johnny Robinson W.	
	J. Darling W.	
	— Pearson W.	
	1894	
Apr 16	Ted Rich W. ko 1	London
Aug 6	John Howley W. 6	Newcastle
	1895	
Feb 3	Joe Smith W. 4	Newcastle
Feb 18	Jerry Driscoll L. 20	N.S.C.
Sep 2	Charlie Johnson L. 17	Newcastle
	1897	
Feb 19	Jem Smith W. Fl. 5 (164-198)	Newcastle
(Smith had stipulated to stop Chrisp in 8 rounds)		
Jun 23	Starlight W. 12	Newcastle
	1898	
Nov 25	Frank Craig L. ko 13	Newcastle
(English Middleweight Title)		
	1901	
Apr 1	Ben Taylor W. ko 8	Gateshead
(English Heavyweight Title)		
May 20	Phil. Jack O'Brien L. ko 11	Newcastle
(English Heavyweight Title)		
	1903	
Feb 23	Jack Mullen L. ko 10	Newcastle
	1906	
Jan 27	Tom Lancaster L. ret. 11	Newcastle

EDDIE CONNOLLY

Born 16 November, 1876.   New Brunswick, Canada.

	1894	
	Peter Manning W. ko 1	
	Peter Manning W. ko 2	
	Danny Smith W. 4	
Dec 13	Johnny Griffin W. 6	St. John
	1895	
Feb 10	Jimmy Dime W. 3	Cleveland
(World 9st. 4lb. Title)		
	Frank Gerzard W. ko 3	
(American 9st. 4lb. Title)		
	Billy Welsh W. 5	
Apr 19	Leslie Pierce D. 15	
Jul 1	Joe Flaherty D. 13	
	Paddy Fenton L. 15	
	Maurice Haggerstrom W. ko 1	
(American 9st. 4lb. Title)		
	1896	
Apr 23	Billy Ernst L. 9	Lynn
Nov 24	Tom Causer W. ko 5	Birmingham
(World 9st. 6lb. Title)		
	1897	
Jan 28	Dick Burge D. 10	Birmingham
(English Welterweight Title)		
Apr 15	Leslie Pierce D. 15	—
Apr 28	George Lavigne L. ko 11	New York
(World Lightweight Title)		
Sep 13	Owen Ziegler L. 20	San Francisco
Dec 17	Dal Hawkins L. ko 14	San Francisco
	1898	
Feb 15	Jimmy Kearns D. 20	Cleveland
Mar 22	Charlie McHugh W. 1	St. John
Jun 23	Jack Robinson D. 12	St. John
Jul 25	Joe Mullins W. f. 2	St. John
Oct 27	Tom Broderick W. 9	Yonkers
Nov 26	George Kerwin D. 20	St. Louis
Dec 17	Jack Bennett D. 15	Toronto
	1899	
Mar 24	Kid McPartland D. 25	New York
Jul 31	Matty Matthews L. 25	Coney Island
—	Spike Sullivan D. 20	—
Oct 27	Matty Matthews W. 25	New York
Dec 15	Kid McPartland W. 25	New York
	1900	
Mar 19	Matty Matthews L. 14	Brooklyn

Apr 19	Jack Twin Sullivan W. f. 8	Boston
May 21	Jack Twin Sullivan D. 15	Boston
Jun 5	Matty Matthews W. 25	Coney Isle
(World Welterweight Title)		
Aug 13	Rube Ferns L. ko 15	Buffalo
Nov 22	Spike Sullivan L. ko 8	New Haven
Nov 29	Owen Ziegler L. ko 2	Hartford
(American Welterweight Title)		
—	Jim Maloney L. 5	—
	1901	
Feb 22	Patsy Sweeney L. 5	Hartford
—	Perry Queenan W.	—
	1902	
Jan 6	Joe Gans L. ko 5	Philadelphia
Jun 21	Pat Daley W. 15	N.S.C.
Jul 19	Jack Palmer L. 20	Newcastle
(English Middleweight Title)		
Aug 23	Jack Palmer L. rsf 7	Newcastle
(English Middleweight Title)		
Sep 15	Tom Woodley L. pts. 11	New Adelphi
(English 10st. 6lb. Title)		
Nov 24	Jack Palmer L. 12	N.S.C.
(English Middleweight Title)		
	1903	
Jan 26	Tom Woodley W. 15	N.S.C.
(English 10st. 6lb. Title)		
Jul 22	Jack Twin Sullivan D. 10	Halifax
Aug 10	Jack Twin Sullivan D. 10	St. John
	1904	
Jan 15	Honey Mellody L. ko 1	Boston
	1905	
Feb 25	Tom Foley nd 6	Chicago
May 4	Packy McFarland L. ko 2	Summit

GEORGE CORFIELD

Born 1873.   Sheffield.

	1890	
Jul 8	Harry Clarke L. 2	Sheffield
	1891	
Feb 20	Harry Clarke W. dis. 2	Sheffield
Oct 5	Bob Fleming W. ko 6	—
Dec 21	Dot Fleming D. 20	Sheffield

	1892	
Jun 9	Frank Kenny L. f. 20	Sanger's Circus
Aug 20	Harry Lowe W. 4	Sanger's Circus
Oct 20	Harry Clarke W. 15	Sheffield
	1893	
Jan 4	W. Wilson W. 14	Sheffield
Apr 22	Joe Morton W. ko 13	Sheffield
Oct 16	Bill Brierley W. 20	Sheffield
Dec 11	Chappie Moran W. 20	Sheffield
(English 7st. 12lb. Title)		
	1894	
May 21	Bill Moore W. 20	Sheffield
(English 7st. 12lb. Title)		
Sep 10	Alf Gower W. ret. 12	Sheffield
(English 7st. 12lb. Title)		
	1895	
May 28	Billy Plimmer L. ko 17	N.S.C.
(English 7st. 12lb. Title)		
Sep 9	Nunc Wallace W. ko 18	Sheffield
(English 8st. Title)		
	1896	
Feb 24	Harry Maurier W. 20	Rotherham
Sep 7	Billy Plimmer L. 20	Sheffield
(English 8st. Title)		
	1897	
Mar —	Paddy Mahoney W. 20	Stalybridge
Dec 13	Jabez White L. ko 5	Birmingham
	1898	
Feb —	George Butler W. ret. 4	Sheffield
Mar 1	Harry Delby W. 8	Sheffield
Mar 8	Jack Walker W. 10	Sheffield
(Final of 8st. Championship Competition)		
Sep 5	Jim Williams L. 12	Sheffield
	1899	
—	George Slark D. 20	N.S.C.
	1900	
—	George Slark L. 20	Haymarket
Apr 2	George Slark W. 20	London
Sep 21	Billy Plimmer D. 20	Stalybridge
	1901	
Feb 13	Andrew Tokell L. ko 4	Newcastle
(English 8st. 2lb. Title)		
Oct 28	Fred Delaney L. pts.	Woolwich

1902
—	Johnny Summers L. 6	—
	Undated Contests	
—	Ike Cohen D. 8	America
—	Alf Gower W. 20	—

FRANK S. CRAIG
'The Coffee Cooler'

Born 1st April, 1870. New York.

1891
Apr 7	Yeamans Fisher W. ko 10	Harlem
May 7	Grant Mack W. 6	Long Isle
Nov 11	George Broad W. ko 2	New York
Nov 30	James Frazer W. ko 1	Stamford

1892
Jan 4	Bill Dunn L. ko 3	Stamford
Feb 6	Bill Davis W. 4	New York
Apr 9	Bill Dunn D. 6	New York
Apr 30	Bill Dunn D. 8	New York
Oct 1	Fred Woods W. 5	New York

1893
—	Joe Butler L. 1	—
Feb 11	Jack Van Houton W. 6	New York
Mar 18	Joe Butler L. 2	Philadelphia
Apr 23	George Gannon W. 6	New York
Jun 12	Billy McCarthy L. 4	Philadelphia
Jun 19	Steve O'Donnell L. 4	Philadelphia
Jul 20	Con Coughlin W. 1	Reading
Nov 25	Billy McCarthy W. 6	New York
Dec 30	Joe Ellingsworth W. ko 7	New York

1894
Feb 7	Dan Creedon L. 4	New York
Feb 17	Dick Baker W. 2	New York
—	Johnny Gorman W. 2	New York
Feb 20	Joe Butler W. 1	Philadelphia
Mar 1	Frank Thompson W. ko 2	New York
Mar 16	Fred Morris W. ko 18	Long Isle
Apr 10	Bill Dunn W. ko 1	New York
Apr 26	Peter Burns W. ko 1	New York
Jun 11	Bill Slavin W. ko 2	Minneapolis
Jul 16	Peter Maher L. ko 2	Boston
Oct 8	John O'Brien W. ko 2	N.S.C.

(English Middleweight Title)

Oct 30	John Donoghue W. ko 1	London
Oct 31	Charles Bennett W. 4	London
Nov 1	J. Tully W. ko 2	London
Nov 2	Tom Montgomery W. ko 1	London
Nov 3	John Donoghue W. ko 1	London
Nov 7	Dan Cleary W. ko 1	London
Nov 11	Bill Cheese W. ko 1	London
Nov 12	Tom Thomas W. ko 1	London
Nov 18	Joe Steers Exh. 4	London
Nov 19	Jack Bogan W. ko 3	London
Nov 20	J. O'Leary W. 2	London
Nov 21	Sam Phillips W. ko 2	London
Nov 22	Charles Bannister W. f. 4	London
Nov 23	Alf Mitchell W. ko 2	N.S.C.

(English Middleweight Title)

| Dec 17 | Ted Pritchard W. ko 1 | London |

(English Middleweight Title)

1895

Jan 9	' Curley ' W. ko 1	Hackney
Jan 10	George Sullivan W. 4	Hackney
Jan 11	Woolf Abrahams W. ko 1	Hackney
Feb 4	Felix Scott "Failed to stop"	Newcastle
Mar 11	Frank Slavin L. ko 1	London
Apr 13	John O'Brien W. ko 1	London
Oct 14	Dan Creedon L. 20	N.S.C.

(English Middleweight Title)

1896

| May 11 | Tom Duggan W. 12 | N.S.C. |

1897

| Mar 17 | Dick O'Brien L. rsf. 2 | Birmingham |

(English Middleweight Title)

1898

| Oct 17 | Aust. Billy Edwards W. ko 12 | London |
| Nov 25 | George Chrisp W. ko 13 | Newcastle |

(English Middleweight Title)

1899

Sep 18	Tommy Ryan L. 10	Coney Isle
Oct 3	Jack Root L. 6	Chicago
Oct 13	Jack Root L. 6	Chicago
Nov 24	Tommy West L. 14	New York

1900

| Sep 10 | George Gardiner L. f. 4 | London |

1901

| Nov 18 | Phil. Jack O'Brien L. f. 7 | N.S.C. |

(English Middleweight Title)

1902

Aug 16	Denver Ed Martin L. rsf 3	Newcastle
Aug 30	Denver Ed Martin L. ko 4	Newcastle

1903

Jun 15	Slouch Dixon D. 12	Wonderland

(Advertised English Heavyweight Title)

Jul 27	Jack Palmer L. 12	Newcastle

(English Heavyweight Title)

1905

Apr 25	Kid Davies W. 10	Neath
Jul 22	Slouch Dixon W. 6	London
Aug 12	Private Casling W. ko 2	London
Aug 26	Charlie Knock W. ko 5	London
Sep 23	Mike Crawley L. 6	London
Oct 19	C. St. Clair W. ko 9	Liverpool

1906

Aug 25	Mike Crawley W. ko 4	London
Sep 8	Charlie Allum W. ko 5	London
Dec 1	Private Casling W. 6	London
Dec 6	Mike Crawley D. 6	London
Dec 10	Peter Brown D. 6	London

1907

Jan 19	Harry Shearing L. 11	London
Mar 9	Seaman Kelly W. 6	Portsmouth
Apr 29	Jack Scales W. 6	London
May 18	Slouch Dixon W. rsf. 3	London
Jun 6	Harry Shearing W. 6	Warley Barracks
Jul 13	Jack Scales L. 6	London
Oct 25	Arthur Bennett W. 6	Dover

1908

Mar 16	Iron Hague L. ko 4	Sheffield
Apr 23	Joe White L. 20	Liverpool
Sep 7	Tom Lancaster L. 20	Newcastle
Nov 14	Bob Brown W. ko 4	Dublin
Dec 21	Tom Lancaster L. 20	Newcastle

1909

Jan 4	Tom Lancaster L. 10	Glasgow
Feb 13	Pat Mulcahy W. 7	Curragh
Apr 12	Tom Spring W. ko 1	Dublin

1910

Jan 1	Fred Drummond W. 6	The Paragon
Jan 8	Joe Mills W. 6	London
Jan 17	Fred Drummond D. 6	London
Jan 24	Seaman Broadbent W. ko 1	London

Jan 27	George West L. 6	London
Jan 29	Dennis Haugh W. 6	London
Feb 14	Charlie Webster W. 1	London
Mar 3	Dido Plumb D. 6	London
Mar 30	Private Casling W. 6	London
Apr 30	Bill Thake W. ko 4	London
Jun 23	Bill Cockayne W. 6	London
Oct 3	Tom Edwards D. 6	London
Oct 19	Pat Kelly W. ko 3	Oxford
Oct 24	Dick Rice L. f. 7	London
	1911	
Aug 12	Fred Drummond L. 7	London
Sep 11	Charlie Bradley W. 6	London
Nov 13	E. Thompson W. 10	Leicester
	1912	
Feb 21	Pat Carroll W. 1	Leicester
May 20	E. Thompson W. ko 13	Loughborough
Jul 11	Gunner Ellis L. ko 3	London
	1922	
Aug 5	Jim Rideout L. 3	Manor Hall

WALTER CROOT

	1892	
Sep 19	Joe Bennett L. 11	Kennington
(English 6st. 8lb. Title)		
	1893	
Mar 6	Bill Bolton L. ko 11	N.S.C.
May 1	Pedler Palmer L. ko 17	N.S.C.
(English 7st. 2lb. Title)		
	1894	
Mar 5	Andrew Wood W. 6	N.S.C.
Apr 16	Bill Bolton W. pts.	London
	1896	
Feb 17	Tom Murray W. 3	N.S.C.
Feb 17	Harry Ware W. 3	N.S.C.
Feb 17	Con Barrett W. 3	N.S.C.
Nov 30	Mike Small W. 11	N.S.C.
(English 7st. 4lb. Title)		
	1897	
—	Ernie Stanton L. 12	—
Dec 6	Jimmy Barry L. ko 20 (7st. 12lb.)	N.S.C.
(World Bantamweight Title)		

GEORGE CUNNINGHAM

Undated Contests

	Bill Chester L. 5	
	Bill Eastwick W. 6	
	Bill Eastwick L. 6	
	Alf Britton W. 9	
	'Ponk' Greenwood W. 7	
	Sam Swainsbury W. 1	
	Tom Beal W. 5	
	Jack Higgins W. 4	
	Mike Tobin W. 2	
	Bill Wood L. 7	Newmarket
	Bill Wood Lost	
	Jack Higgins W. 4	
	Ted Mortimer W. 2	
	Alf Green L. ko 3	London
	Jack Goldswain Won	
	Tom Turner W. 1	
	1894	
Feb 1	Tom Beal Exh.	London
	1895	
Oct 9	Bill Wood L. 4	Newmarket
Dec 25	G. Button Won	London
	1896	
Jan 13	George Gough W. ko 3	London
Mar 12	Dick Pepper W. 6	London
Mar —	Bill Bailey —	Bethnal Green
Apr —	Alf Green W. 8	Edmonton
	1897	
Mar 15	Dave Wallace L. ko 8	N.S.C.
Dec 3	Bill Nolan L. 6	London
	1898	
Jan 24	Darkey Wallace L. 10	London
Feb —	Con Haggerty Won	London
Feb 8	Dick Tiddiman W. 6	London
(Final of 9st. Championship Competition)		
Apr 18	Harry Spurden W. ko 3	London
(Final of 9st. Championship Competition)		
	1899	
Mar 3	Tom Ireland Lost	Wonderland
(English 9st. 6lb. Champion Belt)		
Mar 27	John Jenkins —	N.S.C.
	1900	
Apr 20	Joe Clay W. ko 1	N.S.C.

May 28	Bill Wood W. 8	N.S.C.
Jun 2	Bill Chester Won	Wonderland
(English 9st. 2lb. Title)		
	1901	
Oct 25	Harry Greenfield W. 10	N.S.C.

WILL CURLEY

Born 16th August, 1877.   Newcastle-upon-Tyne.   Died 1973.

	1892	
	Willie Vardy Won	Newcastle
	L. Curtis W. 6	Newcastle
	— Keene Won	Newcastle
(Won 104lb. Competition)		
	1893	
	W. Kirton W. ko 7	
	Tim Kelly W. ko 1	
	Tom Sexton W. 6	Newcastle
	S. Rein W. 6	
	W. Vasty W. 3	
	J. Francis W. ko 1	Newcastle
	Ike Cohen W. 4	Newcastle
(Final 8st. Competition)		
	Tommy Murphy D. 8	
	Bill Sparrow W. 3	Percy Cottage
	Fred Sullivan W. 3	Percy Cottage
	1895	
Feb 18	J. J. Garrity W. rsf 8	Newcastle
May 25	Charlie Beadling L. 20	Newcastle
Jul 29	Joe Farrell W. 9	Newcastle
	1896	
Mar —	Ted Daley W. ret. 8	Gateshead
	1897	
Mar —	Ted Daley W. ret. 2	London
Jun —	Tom Turner W. 20	Gateshead
(English 8st. 3lb. Title)		
Nov 8	Patsy Haley W. 20	Newcastle
(World 8st. 4lb. Title)		
	1898	
Mar —	Aust. Billy Murphy W. ko 12	Newcastle
	1899	
Nov 2	George Dixon L. 25 (122lb.)	New York
(World Featherweight Title)		

1900

Jan 22	Nat Smith W. 20	Newcastle
(English 8st. 10lb. Title)		
Apr 12	Jabez White W. ko 1	Newcastle

1901

Jan 21	Jack Roberts L. ko 7	N.S.C.
(English 9st. Title)		
Mar 11	Sammy Kelly W. f. 7	Newcastle

1902

Feb 3	Jack Roberts W. ko 3	Newcastle
(English 9st. Title)		
May 19	Joe White D. 6	Newcastle
Sep 29	George Dixon D. 15	Newcastle
Nov 8	Billy Barrett W. 15	Newcastle

1903

Nov —	Charlie Bobs L. rsf 3	West Hartlepool
Dec 15	Pedler Palmer W. ko 8	Newcastle
(Match made at 8st. 12lb.)		
Dec 22	George Proctor W. ko 8	Newcastle

P.O. MATTHEW 'NUTTY' CURRAN

Born November, 1882.   County Clare, Ireland.

1909

	P.O. Doran L. 15	Plymouth
	P.O. McNamara W. ko 4	Plymouth
	Young Johnson W. 15	Plymouth
	Jack Ripper W. ko 1	Dublin
May 28	Ben Taylor D. 15	Plymouth
	Herbert Hall W. ko 1	Plymouth
Nov 26	Eddie McGoorty L. 20	Dublin
	Harry Croxton W. ko 4	Plymouth

1910

Jan 14	Gunner Hewitt L. 20	Plymouth
Jan 28	Fred Drummond W. ko 2	Plymouth
Feb 11	Iron Hague W. ko 15	Plymouth
(English Heavyweight Title)		
Apr 15	Fred Drummond W. ko 1	Plymouth
(English Heavyweight Title)		
May 23	Gunner Moir W. f. 2	Mountain Ash
(English Heavyweight Title)		
Jun 28	Cyclone Billy Warren n/c 6	Dublin
Aug 5	Seaman Grant W. ko 2	Plymouth
(English Heavyweight Title)		

Aug 18	Jem Roche W. ko 6	Dublin
(English Heavyweight Title)		
Aug 31	Peter Rice W. ko 1	Plymouth
(English Heavyweight Title)		
Sep 26	Jewey Smith dnc 7 (Belt)	Wonderland
(British Heavyweight Title)		
Oct 30	Jewey Smith W. ko 3	Plymouth
(British Heavyweight Title)		
Nov 18	Alf Langford L. f. 1 (USA)	Plymouth
Dec 12	Gunner Hewitt W. ret. 2	Plymouth
(British Heavyweight Title)		

1911

Jan 18	Bill Lang W. f. 1 (Aust)	London
(Empire Heavyweight Title)		
Feb 24	Dan Porky Flynn L. f. 3 (USA)	Plymouth
Apr —	Jack Scales W. ko 4	Plymouth
(British & Empire Heavyweight Titles)		
May 19	Jack Burns W. ko 14 (USA)	Plymouth
Jun 30	Fred Storbeck n/c 6 (SA)	Plymouth
(Empire Heavyweight Title)		
Aug 4	Herbert Synott W. ko 8	Plymouth
(British & Empire Heavyweight Titles)		
Aug 11	Bill Flynn W. ko 1 (USA)	Plymouth
Sep 15	Bob Scanlan L. f. 3 (USA)	Plymouth
Oct 13	Herbert Roc W. ko 4 (Fr.)	Plymouth
Oct 20	Bob Scanlan L. f. 1	Plymouth
Nov 25	George Gunther D. 20 (Aust)	Paris
Dec 1	Jim Johnson W. f. 4 (USA)	Plymouth
Dec 29	Gunner Healy W. ko 7	Plymouth
(British & Empire Heavyweight Titles)		

1912

Jan 12	Fred Storbeck L. f. 3 (SA)	Plymouth
(Empire Heavyweight Title)		
Feb 21	Kid McCoy L. 20 (USA)	Nice
Feb —	George Gunther L. 10	Nice
Mar 15	George Rodel L. 15 (SA)	Plymouth
Mar 29	George Rodel L. f. 1	Plymouth
Apr 22	Fred Storbeck L. f. 13	London
(Empire Heavyweight Title)		
Aug 12	Gustave Mathuin W. 8 (Fr.)	London
Sep 2	Gunner Moir W. ko 1	London
(British Heavyweight Title)		
Sep 23	George Rodel L. f. 16	London
Nov 16	Herbert Synott W. ko 2	Plymouth
(British Heavyweight Title)		

Dec 6	Gaston Pigot L. f. 9 (Fr.)	Belfast
Dec 20	Dan Voyles L. f. 3 (Irish)	Belfast

(This was Curran's first defeat by a British Boxer since winning the British Heavyweight Title from Iron Hague)

1913

Jan 10	Gunner Ellis W. ko 1	Plymouth
May 3	Bill Lang L. 20	Sydney
Aug 16	Bill Lang L. 20	Sydney
Aug 30	Pat Daran L. f. 2	Melbourne
Nov 28	Harry Smith W. 15 (SA)	Plymouth
Dec 19	Harry Smith W. ko 1	Plymouth

1914

Jan 16	Gunner McMurray W. ko 3	Plymouth
Jan 24	Sam Langford L. ko 1	Paris
Feb 28	Hawker Wilson W. ko 8	Plymouth
Mar 27	— Robur W. ko 6 (Fr.)	Plymouth
Apr 23	Colin Bell W. f. 10 (Aust)	Liverpool
May 8	Kid Jackson W. f. 8 (USA)	Plymouth
May 25	Jim Savage L. 20 (USA)	London
Jun 5	Kid Jackson L. ret. 4	Plymouth
Jul 10	Con O'Kelly L. rsf. 8 (Irish)	Plymouth
Aug 2	Kid McCoy L. 20	London

1915

(No Record)

1916

Mar 31	Bomb. Billy Wells L. ko 5	Plymouth

(British Heavyweight Title)

Dec 8	Dick Rice L. 15	Plymouth

1917

Sep 10	Jack Curphy L. rsf. 3	Holborn

1918

(No Record)

1919

Mar 31	P.O. Smales W. ko 3	London
Apr 21	Eddie McGoorty L. ko 8	Plymouth
Jun 9	Tom Berry L. 15	Plymouth
Oct 10	Fred Fulton L. ret. 4	Plymouth
Oct 18	Seaman Costello W. ko 3	Truro
Nov 5	Arthur Townley L. rsf. 7	Plymouth
Dec 26	Harry Croxon	Bournemouth

1920

Jan 14	Ivor Powell L. 15	Bristol

PAT DALEY

Born 18th July, 1875.   Knocknagoree, Ireland.

	Cock Robin W. 5	
	Cock Robin W. 1	
	Albury Clifford W. 10	
	Jack Fitzpatrick W. 3	
	Johnny Raw Drew	
	Denny Gill Won	
	Jack Ross W. 6	
	Jack Dearsley W. ko 2	
	Jack Ross Drew	
	Casper Leon D. 6	
	Eddie Loader L. pts.	
	Stanton Abbott D. 4	
	Billy Plimmer D. 4	
	Joe McGrath W. 2	
	Jack McGrath W. 3	
	Jack McGrath W. 4	
	1894	
	Jack Gorman W. 2	London
	T. Hearn W. 6	
	Harry King Drew	
	Ted Mortimer W. 7	
	Joe Filkins W. 6	
	Jack Heaseman Won	Derby
	Arthur Callan W. 8	Adelphi Club
	1895	
—	Maurice Phillips W. 5	Holborn
Mar 18	Tommy Harris W. 10	N.S.C.
Mar —	Dummy Winters W. 6	—
Aug 16	Arthur Lock L. 20	Trouville
Oct —	Arthur Lock W. 10	N.S.C.
	1896	
—	Arthur Lock Won	Kennington
Mar 12	Jewey Cooke L. 12	London
—	Jem Richardson W. 1	—
Apr 22	Ted Ware W. 3	Bethnal Green
Apr 23	Joe Anderson W. 4	Bethnal Green
—	Jewey Cooke W. 7	—
Apr 23	Arthur Valentine W. 6	Kennington

May 18	Walter Eyles W. 3	N.S.C.
May 18	Tom Ireland L. 3	N.S.C.
May 22	Arthur Valentine W. 12	London

1897

Jan 25	Billy Hill W. 15	N.S.C.

(World Lightweight Title)

Nov 1	Cock Robin L. 10	London

1898

Oct 12	Owen Sweeney W. 10	Woolwich
Dec 12	Driver Pinchen W. 9	N.S.C.

1899

—	Tom Woodley W. 15	N.S.C.
Aug 10	Aurelio Herrera L. 7	Bakersfield
Oct 12	Aurelio Herrera L. 14	Bakersfield

1900

Feb 20	Jack Scales W. 3	Wonderland
Feb 21	Bill Shaw W. 1	Wonderland
Feb 22	Jem Styles W. ko 1 (55sec.)	Wonderland

(Final of Heavyweight Championship Competition)

1901

Feb 11	Johnny Hughes W. ret. 12	N.S.C.

(English 10st. Lightweight Title)

1902

Jun 21	Eddie Connolly L. 15	N.S.C.

1904

Feb 15	Jack Clancy L. 15	N.S.C.

(English 10st. 6lb. Welterweight Title)

Nov 21	Bobby Dobbs L. 8	Newcastle
Nov 31	Bobby Dobbs L. 15	N.S.C.

1906

Feb 6	Mike Crawley W. ko 5	London
Aug 4	Charlie Knock W. 9	London

1907

Feb 11	Jack Goldswain L. ko 5	N.S.C.

1908

Apr 13	Charlie Knock n/c 7	Sheffield

1911

—	Johnny Lore nd. 4	—

CHARLEY DAVIS
(Michael Davis)

Born 2nd August, 1849.   Stepney.   Died 15th February, 1880.

1872

Feb 1	Abe Daultry W. ret. 2	Kilburn

Feb 1   Bat Mullins W. 3 (£20 Silver Cup)   Kilburn
(Final of 11st. 7lb. Competition)
Feb 9   Obadiah Atterbury W. 3   Whitechapel
Feb 9   Jack Hicks L. 3 (Silver Cup)   Whitechapel
(Final of Featherweight Competition)
Mar 13   Denny Harrington W. 3 (£10 Silver Cup)   London
(Final of 9st. 11lb. Competition)
         1873
Jan 7   John McConnell W. 14r. 88m. (Bow Cup)   London
(English Middleweight Title)
Due to the unsatisfactory ending of the bout, a new rule was
introduced for future bouts with the gloves. This stated that if a
boxer was floored with a punch, he had ten seconds in which to
regain his feet. If he failed to do so he would be "Knocked out of
time".
Apr 21   Ted Napper W. 21r. 84m. (Bow Cup)   Grafton Chapel, Soho
(English Middleweight Title)
         1876
June —   Announced retirement due to ill health.
         1878
Apr 4   Tom Allen L. f. 5r. 18m. 25s. (£200)   Cambridge Heath
(English Heavyweight Title)

ANTHONY DIAMOND

Born 13th November, 1861. Birmingham.   Died 22nd July, 1930.

Won ABA Lightweight Titles, 1883, 1884 & 1885.
Won ABA Heavyweight Title in 1886.
         1887
—   Sam Baxter W. 10   London
         1889
Jan 21   Dick Burge W. 12   Newcastle
—   George Wilson Lost   —
         1890
—   Arthur Bobbett W. ko 10   —
(English 10st. 8lb. Title)
—   H. W. C. Murray Won   —
—   Jimmy Lowe Won   Newcastle
Dec 4   H. King Won   N.S.C.
         1894
Jan 15   Ted White L. 20 (£100)   N.S.C.
(English Middleweight Title)
         1895
Apr 8   Jack Varley W. 12   Birmingham

G

1898
Feb —   John Jackson W. ko 6   Birmingham
Feb 25   Dido Plumb W. 12   Birmingham
(English Middleweight Title)

GEORGE DOVE

Born 1843.   London.   Died December, 1895.

1863
Jan 26   Bill Lead D. 60m. (Police) (£10)   Essex Marshes
(Dove received £4 to draw)
       1867
Jul 3   Wolf Cohen W. 35r. 128½m. (102-118) (£30)   London District
       1872
Jan 23   Alec Lawson L. 2 (Gloves)   London
Feb 8   J. Hickton W. 3   Whitechapel
(Final of Open 116lb. Competition)
Apr 1   George Cunningham W. 3   Soho
Apr 15   Alec Lawson W. 3   Soho
Apr 15   Jerry Hawkes W. 5 (Bow Cup)   Soho
(Final of 8st. 4lb. Championship Competition)
       1877
Aug 8   Jerry Hawkes W. ko 2 (116lb.) (£50 Bow Cup)   London
(English Bantamweight Title)
Aug 8   Bob Habbijam Exh. 3   London

PUNCH DOWSETT

Born 1850.   (5ft. 2in.)

1875
Feb 16   J. Browne W. 3   London
Feb 16   Tim Harrington W. 3   London
Feb 16   Jem Laxton W. 3   London
(Final of Open 9st. 7lb. Competition)
Jul 26   Ben Stocking W. 3   Hackney Wick
Jul 26   Young Cable W. 3 (Silver Cup & £5)   Hackney Wick
(Final of 9st. Competition)
Dec —   Dick Longman Won   —
Dec 28   B. Ellis Won   Shoreditch
Dec 28   — Savage Won   Shoreditch
Dec 28   Bill Green D. 4   Shoreditch
(Final of 9st. 4lb. Competition)

1876
Jan 4   Bill Green W. 3   Shoreditch
(Re-newed Final of 9st. 4lb. Competition)
May 16   Harry Ross W. 15r. 62m. (113-115)   Whitechapel Road
         1877
Mar 12   Bob Laxton Won   Hoxton
Mar 12   James Muskett Won (Silver Cup)   Hoxton
(Final of 8st. 7lb. Competition)
Oct 22   W. Steadman W. 3 (Silver Cup)   Hoxton
(Final of Bill Hundred's 9st. Featherweight Championship Competition)
Dec 11   Tom Hawkins D. 41r. 160m. (108-107½) (£50 Silver Cup)
(English Featherweight Title)   Hoxton
         1878
May —   Joe Fowler Exh.   Bethnal Green
—   Tommy Orange L. 6   'Blue Anchor', Shoreditch

BOYO DRISCOLL

Cardiff.

         1902
Sep 8   Jimmy Exhall W. 6   Cardiff
Sep 15   Jimmy Exall W. 10   Cardiff
Oct 18   Jimmy Rees W. ko 1   Cardiff
Dec 15   Billy Phalin W. ko 5   Cardiff
         1903
Nov 5   Jem Lee L. 2   Dublin
Nov 30   Jack Christian W. 6   N.S.C.
Dec 5   George Moore D. 6   London
         1904
Jan 18   Johnny Hughes W. 10   N.S.C.
Feb 22   Bob Kendrick D. 12   Cardiff
Aug 1   Owen Moran W. 10   Cardiff
(English 8st. Title)
Dec 5   P. Emmanuel W. 20   Cardiff
         1905
Feb 27   Jim Kenrick L. 15   N.S.C.
(English 8st. Title)
Nov 15   Harry Brodigan L. 5   Cardiff
         1906
Oct 29   Darkey Haley L. 7   N.S.C.
         1907
Jan 24   Chris Clarke L. 20   Liverpool
Jun 12   P. Emmanuel W. 4   Cardiff

Dec 14	Harry Sterling W. 6	London
Dec 21	Tom Danahar L. 6	London
	1909	
Feb 18	Frankie Neil nd 10	New York
	1910	
Mar 8	Knockout Brown nd 10	New York
	1911	
Jul 17	Joe Mandot L. 8	Memphis
Oct 23	Charlie White L. 8	Memphis

CHARLIE EXALL

Born 1880. Bermondsey.

	1897	
May 3	Dave Morbin W. 6	N.S.C.
Sep 29	Alf Rosset W. 12	London
Oct —	Harry Brodigan D. 8	London
	1898	
Jan —	Bill Lampshire L. 6	—
Jan 22	Bill Dixon W. 6	Bethnal Green
Jan 22	Albert Hollins W. 6	Bethnal Green
Jan 22	Wag Hampton L. 6	Bethnal Green
Feb 26	Bill Stonelake L. 6	London
—	Jack Walker W. 20	London
(English 7st. 10lb. Title)		
Apr 4	Harry Brodigan W. f. 17	Gateshead
(English 7st. 6lb. Title)		
Oct 30	Wag Hampton W. 6	London
Nov 28	Mike Riley L. 20	N.S.C.
(English 7st. 6lb. Title)		
	1899	
Apr 1	Harry McDermott L. ko 14	Gateshead
(English 7st. 8lb. Title) (Exall 3lb. Overweight)		
May 29	Mike Riley W. rsf 19	Gateshead
(English 7st. 6lb. Title)		
	1900	
Apr 16	Harry McDermott L. 12	Newcastle
Jun —	Harry Slough W. 6	Kennington
	1901	
Jun —	Kid Veitch Won	—
Jul 22	Harry McDermott L. 20	Gateshead
(English 7st. 10lb. Title)		

Nov 4	Matt Precious W. ko 6	Newcastle

(English 7st. 8lb. Title)
1902
Feb 10 Jack Walker W. 20 — London
(English 7st. 8lb. Title)
Aug 2 Dot Elder L. 8 — Newcastle
Sep 27 Harry McDermott W. ret. 8 — Newcastle
(Match made at 7st. 8lb. 2-minute rounds)
1903
Jan 17 Jim Kenrick D. 15 — Newcastle
(World & English 7st. 8lb. Titles)
Feb 23 Jim Kenrick L. 20 — Newcastle
(World & English 7st. 8lb. Titles)
Dec 19 Ernest Goodwin W. ko 5 — Newcastle
1905
Oct 12 Jim Kenrick L. ko 8 — Liverpool
1911
Mar 20 Harry McDermott W. 15 — South Shields
Undated Contests
1902 Jim Kenrick L. 20 — —
— Tom Snow L. 6 — —
— Tom Snow L. 8 — —

JACK FITZPATRICK

Born 1867.

1892
Nov 25 Tom Wilson W. 8 — Manchester
1893
Feb 20 Tom Wilson W. 14 — Manchester
Oct 2 Charlie Tilley W. 9 — N.S.C.
Nov 3 Tom Lynch W. 5 — Dublin
1895
Feb 6 Harry Spurden W. 7 — Clapham Junction
(English 9st. Title)
1900
— — Roach L. ko 4 — Dublin
Undated Contest
— Pat Daley L. 3 — —

JEM GAIGER

1878

Feb 13	F. Kent W. 3	London
Apr 3	T. King W. 3	Finsbury
Apr 3	W. Jenkins W. ret. 3	Finsbury
Apr 6	H. Edwards W. ret. 3	Finsbury

(Final of Middleweight Competition)

Apr —	J. Clow W. ret. 2	Finsbury
Apr 24	George Rivett W. 3	Finsbury

(Final of Heavyweight Champions Cup Competition)

Dec 11	W. Goodfellow W. 3	London
Dec 11	Jack Burke W. 3	London

(Final of Middleweight Competition)

1880

Feb 12	Jack Burke D. 35m. (Knuckles)	Hackney Marshes

(English Middleweight Title)

TOM GARDNER
(Thomas Edwin Gardner)

Born 27th June, 1869.   St. George's, London.   (5ft. 1½in.)

Died January, 1946.

	Won Competition	Mason Arm, Bow Common
	Won Competition	Nottingham
	Goody Jacobs Won	
	Con Donovan Won	

1887

Jun 15	T. Commons Won	St. George's Boxing Club
Jun 15	D. Clark Won	St. George's Boxing Club
Jun 15	J. Bennett Lost	St. George's Boxing Club

(Final of 8st. 4lb. Competition)

Sep 22	T. Yarnton L. 2	Whitechapel

1888

Oct 4	Harry Saphir D. 31r. 158m.	—

1889

Feb —	Wag Stevens Exh.	Bethnal Green
Mar 9	W. Beach Won	Holloway
Mar 9	Fred Sullivan Won	Holloway
Mar 9	Sam Milner Won	Holloway

(Final of 8st. Competition)

Mar 21	Jack Hullett Won	Lambeth
Apr 6	Fred Sullivan W. 10	—

Oct 9	Ted Jones W. 6	Newmarket
Oct 14	Charlie Mansford W. 12	Westminster
Dec 3	Arthur Carpenter W. 3	London
Dec 3	G. Mendoza Won	London
Dec 3	J. H. Ramplin Lost	London
	1890	
Jan 1	Charlie Mansford W. 6	Kennington
Feb 18	Bill Goode W. 18	Kennington
May 28	Arthur Wilkinson L. 27	Kennington
Nov 19	Dave Cable Exh. 6	Shoreditch
Dec 18	Tom Walker Won	Kennington
Dec 18	Charlie Mansford Lost	Kennington
	1891	
Jan 15	Jem Stevens Exh.	Shoreditch
Nov 4	Charlie Mansford W. 11	—
	1892	
Jan 28	Nunc Wallace W. f. 11	Kennington
(English 8st. 2lb. Title)		
Oct 5	Willie Smith L. ko 10	Kennington
(English 8st. 2lb. Title)		

BILL GOODE 'Chesterfield'

Born 16th April, 1864.   London.   (5ft. 7½in.)

	1882	
	Fred Walker Won	London
	1883	
Jan 19	Owen Hannan Lost (Competition)	Mile End
Nov 19	Dick Roberts D. 9r. 33m. 22s. (Police)	London
Nov 27	Dick Roberts W. 83r. 93m.	—
	1884	
Feb 2	Pat Perry W. 33r. 65m. (152-140)	Chingford
	1885	
Jan 1	John Barry D. 2r. (Police)	Cheshunt
—	Alec Roberts Lost (Competition)	London
	1886	
May 7	Jim Kendrick D. 20r. 78m. (Police)	Lambeth
	1887	
Aug 30	Tom Lees W. 15r. (154lb.) (£100)	Lambeth
(Generally Recognised as the Middleweight Champion)		
Oct 15	Tom Lees D. 5r. (Ring Broken)	Brewer Street
	1888	
Apr 14	Ted Burchell Won	Islington

Nov —	Arthur Bobbett W. 12 (150-152)	Manchester
	1889	
Apr 24	Ted Burchell W. 3	Wood Green
Apr 27	Ted O'Neil W. ret. 1	London
	(Final of Heavyweight Championship Competition)	
Oct 17	Frank Slavin L. ko 5	London
	1890	
Feb 8	Charles Toff Wall L. 12	Pelican Club
	(English Middleweight Title)	
	1898	
May 20	Arthur Akers L. rsf 2	N.S.C.

ALF GREENFIELD

Born 1853.   Northampton.

1877

Apr —   Pat Perry L. 17r. 40m. (Police) (147-   )

Beggar Bush, Nr. Sheffield

1878

Apr 28   Sam Breeze W. 56m. (£50)   Tamworth
May 19   Jemmy Highland W. 60m.   Packington

1879

Jul 21   Jemmy Highland W. f. 16m. (148-126) (£200 Cup)

Bingley Hall, Birmingham

Nov 28   Denny Harrington L. f. 18r. 70½m. (150-168) (£50 Cup)
(World & English Middleweight Titles)   London

1880

Feb 25   Jem Stewart W. f. 20r. 83m. (£100)   Chelsea
(Claimed English Heavyweight Title)

1881

May —   Tug Wilson D. 21r. 85m.   —
(English Heavyweight Title)

1882

Jun 28   M. Galligan Won   —

1883

Jan 13   William Sheriff Exh. 3   Birmingham
Jun 29   Jack Burke W. 3 (Jem Mace's Belt)   Manchester
(Final of All-Weights Championship Competition)

1884

Nov 17   John L. Sullivan 2r. (Police)   New York

1885

Jan 12   John L. Sullivan L. 4   Boston
Feb 27   George Fryer D. 4   —

| Mar 2 | Jack Burke L. 5 | Chicago |
| Mar 23 | Jack Burke D. 7 | Chicago |

1886

Feb 17 Jem Smith D. 13r. 55m. (Knuckles)   Maison-laffite
(English Heavyweight Title)

HARRY GREENFIELD

Born 1873.   Camden Town, London.

1889?

— Bill Corbett L. 25   —
(English 8st. 10lb. Title)

1891

— G. Cowlett W. ko 2   —
— Jack Webb W. ko 2   —

1892

May 16 Charles Tilley L. 20   —

1893

May 12 Bill McGrath W. f. 4   Kennington

1894

Feb 12 Sam Sorrell W. rsf 7   N.S.C.
Oct 6 Tom Causer L. 11   London

1895

Feb 11 Harry Callum W. 10   N.S.C.
Apr 23 Joe Anderson W. 6   N.S.C.

1896

Feb 24 Tom Ireland W. 11   N.S.C.
Nov 9 Jem Curran W. ko 9   Sheffield

1897

Jan 11 Fred Johnson W. ko 13   London
(English Featherweight Title)
Mar 3 Larry Barnes W. ko 8   Birmingham
(World 9st. Title)

1898

Feb 23 Spike Sullivan L. ko 15   N.S.C.
(World 9st. Title)

1899

May 29 Ben Jordan L. ko 9   N.S.C.
(English 8st. 12lb. Title)
Nov 30 Jabez White L. ko 8   London
(English 9st. 2lb. Title)
— Joe Anderson W. 8   —
— Darkey Barton Won   Kennington

	1900	
Mar 25	Tom Ireland L. ko 11	London
Apr 26	Tom Ireland L. ko 8	Wonderland
—	Tom Ireland W. 10	—
	1901	
Oct 25	George Cunningham L. 10	N.S.C.
	1902	
Jan 29	Bob Russell L. 6	Wonderland

ROBERT HABBIJAM

(Recognised as English Lightweight Champion until 1880)

	1876	
Mar 18	T. Sturk W. 3	Islington
Mar 18	Lumpy Hughes W. 3	Islington
Mar 18	Jem Laxton W. 3	Islington
(Final of World Ten Stone Championship Competition)		
Mar 27	Jem Laxton L. 3	Rotherhithe
(Final of Lightweight Competition)		
Apr —	Soldier W. Robinson L. 3	London
	1877	
Aug 8	George Dove Exh. 3	London

YOUNG HUNDREDS
(William Pulham)

Born 1844.   Hoxton.

—	Bill Alexander Won (Turn-up)	—
—	Harry Meads Won (£20)	—
	1865	
Nov 8	Bill Crane W. 175m. (£20)	London District
	1867	
—	Tim Collins Won by knockout (Gloves)	London
Oct 23	Alec Lawson D. 99r. 235m. (Police) (£50)	London District
	1872	
Jan 23	Tom Goller W. 2	Soho
Jan 23	Alec Lawson D. 2 (Silver Cup)	Soho
(Final of Open 8st. 7lb. Competition)		
Apr 1	A. McCormack W. 3	Soho
Apr 15	Jerry Hawkes L. 3	Soho
(Semi-final of 8st. 4lb. Championship Cup Competition)		
Winner of 8st. 8lb. Champion's Cup		
Dec 20	Presented with the Lightweight Championship Belt. (9st.)	

TOM IRELAND

	Undated Contests	
	Jack Farley W. 8	—
	Jack Farley L. 24	Kennington
	Jack Farley L. 11	Squire Abingdon's Estate
	Ted Ware W. 9	—
	Ted Ware W. 6	Tom Symonds
	Ted Ware L. 10	Camden Town
	Ted Ware Lost	—
	Darkey Barton L. 8	—
	Charlie Wilson L. 6	—
	Bill Corbett Won	—
	Jack Fitzgibbons Won	—
	1893	
Dec 26	Darkey Barton W. 20	Leeds
	1894	
Apr —	Tom Causer L. 11	London
	1895	
Sep 23	Ted Ware W. 3	N.S.C.
Oct —	Arthur Lock L. 3	London
Dec 2	Dave Wallace W. 15	N.S.C.
	1896	
Jan 13	Archie Phillips Won	N.S.C.
Jan 13	Harry Webster Won	N.S.C.
Jan 13	Ted Ware W. 3	N.S.C.
(Final of 9st. 8lb. Competition)		
Feb 11	Harry Greenfield L. 11	N.S.C.
May 18	Harry Webster W. 3	N.S.C.
May 18	Pat Daley W. 3	N.S.C.
May 18	Alf Bannister W. 3	N.S.C.
Dec —	Tom Causer L. 6	Birmingham
	1897	
Feb 8	Harry Spurden W. 10	N.S.C.
Mar —	Walter Eyles W. 6	Holborn
Apr —	Joe Anderson L. 6	Bethnal Green
(Final of 9st. 8lb. Champion's Belt Competition)		
May 17	Charlie Meacock W. pts. 11	N.S.C.
Dec —	T. F. Davison W. rsf 6	N.S.C.
	1898	
Mar 25	Dave Wallace L. ko 20	N.S.C.
	1899	
Mar 3	Alf Bannister Won	Wonderland
Mar 3	George Cunningham Won	Wonderland
(Final of 9st. 6lb. Champion Belt Competition)		

Apr 2	Ted Ware D. 10	Northampton
Dec 12	Jack Roberts W. 5	N.S.C.
	1900	
Mar 25	Harry Greenfield W. ko 11	London
Apr 26	Harry Greenfield W. ko 8	Wonderland
—	Harry Greenfield L. 10	—
Aug 2	Jack Goldswain W. 2	Wonderland
(English 9st. 6lb. Title)		
Sep 3	Jack Everhardt L. f. 10	Wonderland
(English 10st. Title)		
	1901	
Oct 28	Charlie Knock W. 6	London
	1902	
Feb 12	Ted Ware n/c 5	Wonderland
Mar 9	Jim Maloney L. 10	N.S.C.
May 3	Charlie Knock L. 6	London
Nov 24	Charlie Knock L. 6	London
—	Walter Eyles L. 6	—

ANDREW JEPTHA

Born 30th December, 1879.   Cape Town.

	1899	
	Beyers Won	
	Bergman Won	
	Areudse Won	
	1902	
Sep 11	Jim Green L. rsf 12	Liverpool
—	Dick Ward L. ko 2	Liverpool
	1904	
Feb 8	Sid Doyle W. ko 2	Marylebone
Feb 29	Sid Doyle W. 1	Marylebone
Mar 14	Jack Kingsland L. 6	Marylebone
Jun 16	Charlie Knock L. 2	Plaistow
Jul 30	Jack Andrews W. ko 5	Wonderland
Aug 13	Jack Scales L. 6	Wonderland
Oct 3	Joe Platford D. 6	N.S.C.
Dec 2	Jack Costello L. 6	Birmingham
	1905	
Aug 31	Charlie Hickman L. 12	Liverpool
Nov 6	Joe Halligan L. 3	Liverpool
	1906	
Feb 1	Jack Dunleary W. 2	Liverpool

Nov 3	Sid Doyle W. ko 2	Wonderland
Nov 17	Harry Sharper W. ko 3	Wonderland
Nov 21	Gunner Hart W. 3	Walsingham
Nov 24	Curley Watson L. 10	Wonderland
	1907	
Jan 30	Young John L. Sullivan W. 9	Waterford
Feb 11	Curley Watson L. 20	Wonderland
(English Welterweight Title)		
Feb 27	Julien Dupont L. 10	Paris
Mar 25	Curley Watson W. ko 4	Wonderland
(English Welterweight Title)		
Aug 8	Joe White L. 15	Merthyr
(English Welterweight Title)		
Sep 19	Dave Peters W. ko 10	Aberdare
Nov 18	Curley Watson L. 15	N.S.C.
	1908	
Feb 24	Tom Lancaster L. 20	Newcastle
Jun 26	Young Joseph D. 20	Birmingham
Nov 7	Joe Smith W. ko 10	Paris
	1909	
Jan 25	Alf Hewitt W. 13	Wonderland
Mar 22	Bart Connelly L. 15	N.S.C.
May 26	Willie Lewis L. ko 3	Charing Cross
Jun 23	Tom Lancaster L. 15	Newcastle
Aug 21	Joe Heathcote W. f. 7	Wigan
Oct 8	P.O. Doran L. 9	Plymouth
Nov 29	Harry Duncan D. 6	London
	1910	
Jun 20	Dave Peters L. 2	Mountain Ash
Jul 21	Joe White n/c 2	Liverpool
	Retired	

FRED JOHNSON

Born 3 October, 1865.   Hackney, London.

	1884	
Won All-Comers Competition		Hackney
	Bill Hook D. 4	Shoreditch
(Final of 9st. Competition)		
	Bill Hook L. 4	Mile End
	1886?	
	Dido Hopwood Won	Whitechapel
(Final of 8st. 6lb. Championship Belt)		

	Dave Burke W. 4	London
(Lightweight Competition)		
	Bill Baxter Won	Snaresbrook
(£10 Competition)		
Won £15 Competition		Haymarket
	1888	
Apr 10	Tom Euston W. 4	London
Apr —	Reuben Baxter W. 6	London
Apr 14	Pudsey Sullivan W. 4	London
(Final of Ben Hyam's 8st. 10lb. Competition)		
—	Bill Cheese W. 9	—
—	Bill Baxter W. 3	London
—	Hippy Homer W. 3	Liverpool
(Final of 8st. 6lb. Championship Competition)		
—	Evan Davies W. 12	Haymarket
Dec —	Bill Baxter W. 4	Wood Green
(Final of Ben Hyam's 8st. 10lb. Competition)		
Dec 21	Bill Baxter L. ret. 42	London
(English Bantamweight Title)		
	1889	
Mar 16	Bill Baxter W. 4	London
(Final of Ben Hyam's 8st. 10lb. Competition)		
—	Bill Baxter W. 6	—
Apr 23	Billy Reader L. 3	Wood Green
Apr 25	Harry Denny W. 3	Wood Green
Oct 20	Tommy Walker W. 3	Haymarket
	1890	
Feb 11	Tom Woolley W. ko 3	Kennington
Mar 31	Bill Baxter L. f. 6	Haymarket
Apr 7	Bill Baxter W. 20	Haymarket
Dec 5	Stanton Abbott W. 4	Kennington
(English 9st. Title)		Kennington
	1891	
Aug 15	James Howe W. f. 10	Walworth
(English 8st. 10lb. Title)		
	1892	
Jun 27	George Dixon L. ko 14	Coney Isle
(World 8st. 5lb. Featherweight Title)		
	1893	
Apr 11	Morgan Crowther L. ko 20	London
(Match made at 8st. 12lb.)		
	1894	
Mar 2	Bill Baxter W. 6	Kennington
May 7	Dave Wallace W. ko 14	N.S.C.
(English 9st. Title)		

	1895	
Apr —	Bill Cheese Won	—
Apr 29	Charlie Beadling W. ko 4	Newcastle
(English 8st. 8lb. Title)		
	1897	
Jan 11	Harry Greenfield L. ko 13	London
(English Featherweight Title)		
Feb 22	Ben Jordan L. ko 12	N.S.C.
(English 8st. 7lb. Title)		
—	Bill Cheese W. pts.	Edgeware Rd.
Dec 16	Darkey Barton	—
	1898	
Feb 17	Harry Spurden L. 3	London
	1901	
Jan 5	Harry Spurden L. ko 2	—

BEN JORDAN

Born 1st April, 1873. Mitcham, Surrey. Died 18th January, 1945.

	1892-94 Undated Contests	
	Dave Wallace L. pts. 9	N.S.C.
	Dave Wallace W. 6	Holborn
	Alf Buckingham W. 1	
	Harry Munroe W. 1	
	George Murray W. 2	
	Jack Welland W. 2	
	Bert Smith W. 3	
	W. C. Wood W. 3	
	Sid Phillips Won	
	Snipe Reynolds W. 2	
	Tom Cooper W. ko 4	London
	Curley Perrin W. 4	
	Tiny Bishop W. 4	
	Alf Johnson W. ret. 6	Marylebone
	George Murray L. 9	
	Bill Connelly Won	
	Bill Connelly Won	
	Bill Connelly Won	
	1894	
Jan 20	Ted Marsh W. 3	N.S.C.
Oct 29	Darkey Wallace W. 6	N.S.C.
	1895	
—	Frank Scott W. ko 10	—
Oct 28	Jim Gough W. ko 3	N.S.C.

1896

Feb 12	Charlie Meacock W. ko 10	London
Apr 22	Alf Barton W. ret. 2	Bethnal Green
Apr 23	George Woods W. 3	Bethnal Green
(Won 8st. 10lb. Competition)		
Jun 2	Joe Portley W. ko 19	London

1897

Feb 27	Fred Johnson W. rsf 12	N.S.C.
(English 8st. 7lb. Featherweight Title)		
Nov 29	Tommy White W. f. 19	N.S.C.
(English 9st. Featherweight Title)		

1898

Apr 4	Eddie Curry W. ret. 17	N.S.C.
(World & English 8st. 10lb. Title)		
Jul 1	George Dixon W. 25	New York
(World 8st. 10lb. Featherweight Title)		
Jul 8	Eldred McCloskey nd 6	Philadelphia

1899

May 29	Harry Greenfield W. ko 9	N.S.C.
(World & English 8st. 12lb. Featherweight Titles)		
Oct 10	Eddie Santry L. ko 16	New York
(World Featherweight Title)		

1900

Apr 23	Bill Fielder D. 6	N.S.C.

1902

May 28	Tommy Hogan W. ko 4	N.S.C.
(English Featherweight Title)		
Jun 23	Kid McFadden W. ko 15	N.S.C.
(World 8st. 8lb. Title)		
Oct 20	Jack Roberts W. ko 5	N.S.C.
(English 9st. Featherweight Title)		

1903

May 2	George Dixon W. 6	London
May 11	George Dixon W. 6	London

1904

Dec 12	Pedler Palmer W. 15	N.S.C.
(English Featherweight Title)		
Dec 29	Frankie Howe nd 3	New York

1905

Jan 5	Harry Shea nd 3	New York
Retired		

JIM KENRICK

Born 15th July, 1882.   London.

Bill Radley W. ko 4
Harry Slough W. ko 8
Buck Shine W. ko 4
Buck Shine W. ko 4
Buck Shine W. ko 4
Bill Green W. 10
Bill Ray W. 3
Jim Exall W. 8
1899

Oct 13   Herbert Rix W. 10   N.S.C.
Jim Exall W. 10
Jim Exall W. 10
Jim Richardson W. 6
Alfred Rosser W. 6
Harry Ashley W. 6
Joe Kenny W. 6
George Collins W. 6
George Collins W. 6
Dave Morbin W. 6
Dave Morbin W. 6
Bill Radley W. 6
Buck Shine W. 4
Bill Bruce W. 6
George Smith W. 6
George Collins W. 6
Dave Morbin W. 6
Ike Bradley W. 15
Young Conroy W. 10
Charlie Dixon W. 10
Joe Eagan W. 6
Young Smith W. 6
Young Smith W. 6
Bob Howard D. 11
Harry Churchill D. 6
Harry Churchill D. 6
Darkey Haley D. 6
Jim Stroud L. 6
Andrew Newton L. rsf 9

H

	Bob Howard W. ko 3	
	Bill Easy W. ko 1	
	1900	
Jan 12	Jim Weston W. ko 2	London
	George Denny W. ko 3	
	Jim Thomas W. ko 2	
	Jim Stroud W. ko 2	
	Jack Maloney W. ko 3	
	Jim Cary W. ko 4	
	Jim Cary W. ko 1	
	Joe Kenny W. ko 6	
	Alf Lloyd W. ko 2	
	Jim Murray W. ko 4	
	Ted Calder W. ko 2	
	Fred Herring W. ko 1	
—	Bill Veitch W. ko 14	Gateshead
(English 7st. 6lb. Title)		
Oct 1	Jim Stroud L. 6	
	1901	
Jan 31	Toby McKenzie W. 8	
	Charlie Smirkes W. 6	
	Jack Fitzpatrick W. 6	
	Jack Fitzpatrick W. 6	
Apr 1	Bill Pike W. 6	Stamford Hill
May 25	George Collins W. 6	London
Sep 28	Jack Christian W. 6	Woolwich
Oct 12	Jim Sweeney W. ko 3	Woolwich
Oct 21	Jack Guyon W. 6	N.S.C.
Oct 29	George Collins W. 8	Newmarket
Nov 2	Harry Smith W. ko 8	Woolwich
Nov 7	Jack Guyon L. 6	London
Nov 23	Dave Morbin W. 6	Woolwich
Dec 7	Jack Guyon L. 6	Woolwich
	1902	
Jan 18	Harold Root L. 4	N.S.C.
Mar 13	Johnny Summers W. 6	Woolwich
Mar 29	Digger Stanley L. 6	London
Apr 21	Dave Job W. 15	N.S.C.
(English 8st. Title)		
May 12	Owen Moran L. 10	N.S.C.
(English 100lb. Title)		
Jun 2	Jack Guyon L. 10	N.S.C.
Sep 6	Tibby Watson W. 6	Woolwich
Sep 8	Harry Churchill W. 6	London

—	Charlie Exall W. 20	—
Oct 22	Jack Walker L. 15	Marylebone
Nov 15	Harry McDermott L. 15	Newcastle
	1903	
Jan 17	Charlie Exall D. 15	Newcastle
Feb 21	Charlie Exall W. 20	Newcastle
(English 7st. 8lb. Title)		
Mar 14	Digger Stanley L. 6	London
Jun 15	Tibby Watson W. 6	London
Sep 14	Young Joseph L. 12	London
Nov 16	Bert Stark W. 10	Hackney
	1904	
Jan 25	Fred Herring W. 15	N.S.C.
Mar 14	Jim Glover W. ko 3	N.S.C.
May 30	Dave Job W. ko 12	N.S.C.
Nov 5	Jack Wren L. 6	London
	1905	
Feb 27	Boyo Driscoll W. 15	N.S.C.
(English 8st. Title)		
Apr 10	Ike Bradley W. 15	N.S.C.
May 4	Ike Bradley D. 20	Liverpool
May 25	Johnny Hughes W. ko 16	Woolwich
Jul 27	Ike Bradley W. 20	Liverpool
Aug 24	Owen Moran L. ko 7	Liverpool
(English 7st. 7lb. Title)		
Sep 23	Harry Homes W. ko 3	Woolwich
Oct 12	Charlie Exall W. ko 8	Liverpool
Oct 19	Jack Fox L. 6	Worcester
Nov 27	Jack Guyon W. 15	N.S.C.
	1906	
Apr 2	Mark Verrall L. 3	N.S.C.
Nov 5	Ginger Osborne W. 10	N.S.C.
	1907	
Jan 7	Sam Keller D. 10	London
Jan 17	Sam Keller L. 6	London
Jan 26	Ted Moore L. 6	Woolwich
Feb 21	Dave Morbin W. 6	Colchester
Oct 5	Harry Smith W. 6	London
Nov 28	Johnny Hughes W. 6	Camberwell
	1908	
Jan 16	Harry Brodigan W. ko 7	Liverpool
Jan 20	Jim Southway W. 15	Merthyr
Feb 22	Harry Norton W. 4	Merthyr
Mar 20	Harry Ware D. 15	Merthyr

Apr 19	Young Smith D. 6	Hoxton
May 9	Jack Veitch W. ko 3	London
May 30	Albert Dabbs W. ko 5	London
Jun 13	Buck Shine W. ko 3	London
Jun 22	Kid Saxby W. ko 6	Birmingham
Jul 1	Harry Ware W. 8	Birmingham
Jul 18	Bill Lewis L. 6	London
Nov 30	Frank McFoy L. 6	London
Dec 19	Tom Smith W. 10	Birmingham
Dec 28	Frank McFoy L. 15	London
	1909	
Apr 3	Harry Ware L. 15	Merthyr
Apr 10	Boyo Bradley W. ko 8	Merthyr
Apr 15	Sam Kellar D. 6	Hackney
Jun 26	Young Pierce nd 6	Philadelphia
Jul 2	Mike Malone nd 6	Philadelphia
Aug 4	Johnny Daly nd 10	New York
Aug 6	Patsy Brannigan nd 10	New York
	1910	
Feb 19	Johnny Coulon L. 10	New Orleans
(World Bantamweight Title)		
Mar 6	Johnny Coulon L. ko 19	New Orleans
(World Bantamweight Title)		
Apr 2	Patsy Brannigan D. 10	New Orleans
Apr 22	Patsy Brannigan D. 10	New Orleans
Sep 12	Johnny Coulon L. 20	London
	1911	
—	Johnny Hughes L. 20	London
—	Joe Shugrue nd 10	New York
May 12	Young Waggoner nd 10	New York
Aug 3	Patsy Brannigan L. 20	Springfield
Aug 30	Bobby Reynolds nd 6	Philadelphia
Oct 11	Young Britt L. ko 10	Baltimore
Dec 11	Jimmy Walsh nd 10	New York
	1912	
Jan 8	Monte Attell nd 6	Pittsburgh
Mar 14	Frankie Burns L. 10	New Orleans
Aug 20	Frankie Burns nd 10	Rockaway
Oct 5	Frankie Conley nd 6	Philadelphia
Dec 14	Frankie Burns nd 10	Brooklyn
	1913	
Jun 11	Kid Williams L. ko 6	Baltimore
Jul 7	Frankie Burns L. ko 9	Rockaway
Sep 2	Jimmy Walsh nd 10	New York
	(Not Complete Record)	

JOHN KNIFTON
'The 81-Tonner'

Born 22nd January, 1855. St. Cyrus, Scotland. (6ft. 1½in.)

Died 6th May, 1896.

1877		
May 12	Jem Madden W. ko 2	London
May 19	Walter Watson W. ko 1	London
May 19	Tom Tully W. 3 (Silver Cup)	London
(Final of World Heavyweight Championship Competition)		
Aug 29	Tom Scrutton W. 9r. (198-210)	London
(English Heavyweight Title)		
1878		
?	Jack Massey W. 39r. 41m. (Knuckles)	Pulborough
1882		
—	Woolf Bendoff W. 3	—
Dec 21	Coddy Middings L. 3	London
1883		
Jan 3	Roger Wallis D. 3	London
—	Charlie Mitchell Exh. 5m.	London
1887		
Feb —	Charles 'Toff' Wall L. 3	London
(Final of Catchweights Competition)		

CHARLIE KNOCK

Born 18th August, 1880. London.

1899		
Jan 9	Alf Rodgers L. 9	Sheffield
1901		
Feb 18	Jack Goldswain L.2	N.S.C.
Mar 23	Bert Firmin W. 1	London
May 4	Jack Fairclough W. 6	London
Oct 12	Ted Ware L. 6	London
Oct 28	Tom Ireland L. 6	London
1902		
Apr 14	Peter Brown W. 6	London
Apr 19	Ernie Veitch D. 8	London
May 3	Tom Ireland W. 6	London
May 12	Peter Brown L. 10	N.S.C.
—	Harry Wade W. 1	—
—	Charlie Ryder W. 1	—
Oct 18	Ernie Veitch W. 6	London

Nov 24	Tom Ireland W. 6	London
Dec 20	Dave Barry L. 6	London
	1899-1902	
	Joe Lee Won	N.S.C.
	Jim Jackson Won	N.S.C.
	Walter Rance Won	N.S.C.
	Jim Turner Won	N.S.C.
(Final of 10st. Competition)		
	Willie Stone Won	
	George Jackson Won	
(Final of 10st. Competition)		
	Tom Dixon W. 3	
	Billy Bell W. ko 8	Newcastle
	Billy Gordon W. 7	
	Billy Johnson W. 5	
	Ted Ware W. 6	
	Alf Wall W. 2	
	Ernie Veitch D. 6	
	Jewey Cooke D. 8	
	Percy Laycock D. 10	
	Ted Ware D. 8	
	1903	
Apr 25	Tom Woodley W. ko 4	London
Sep 12	Charlie Allum W. 6	London
Nov 16	Charlie Allum L. ko 9	London
(English Welterweight Title)		
	1904	
Feb 1	Charlie Allum W. 12	London
(English Welterweight Title)		
Mar 19	Dave Barry W. ko 3	London
Jun 16	Andrew Jeptha W. ko 2	Plaistow
Jul 11	Jack Kingsland W. 6	Barking
Jul 16	Peter Brown W. ko 1	London
Sep 26	Young Peter Jackson L. ko 3	London
(World Welterweight Title)		
	1905	
Feb 20	Tom Woodley L. f. 5	Wonderland
(English 10st. 4lb. Title)		
Apr 1	Jack Scales W. 6	London
May 20	Mike Crawley L. 5	London
Jun 10	Mike Crawley L. 6	London
Aug 26	Frank Craig L. ko 5	London
Oct 7	Peter Brown W. 6	London
Oct 9	Gunner Hart W. 3	London

1906

Jan 27	Billy Edwards W. 6	London
Mar 10	Jem Courtney W. ko 3	London
Mar 17	Jewey Cooke L. 6	London
Apr 21	Curley Watson L. 6	London
May 21	Curley Watson W. rsf 17	London
(English Welterweight Title)		
Aug 4	Pat Daley L. 9	London
Sep 27	Bobby Dobbs L. 9	Liverpool
Nov 10	Curley Watson L. 10	London
(English Welterweight Title)		
Dec 8	Iron Hague W. ko 3	Doncaster
Dec 15	Curley Watson L. 10	London

1907

Jan 12	Billy Edwards W. ko 4	London
Mar 11	H. Fellowes W. 20	Sheffield
May 11	Jack Scales W. 6	London
Jun 8	L/Cpl Baker W. 3	London
Aug 31	Alan Harmon W. 6	London
Sep 28	Alan Harmon L. 6	London
Oct 28	H. Fellowes W. 3	Sheffield
Dec 4	Peter Brown W. ko 11	Paris
Dec 9	Jack Costello L. 6	Sheffield

1908

Mar 2	Peter Brown L. 4	Paris
Apr 13	Pat Daley N/C 7	Sheffield
Apr 18	Curley Watson L. 10	London
(English 10st. 8lb. Championship Belt)		
Aug 1	Jim Sullivan W. ko 4	London
Aug 22	Wag Marshall W. ko 2	London
Aug 29	Jim Sullivan W. 4	London
Sep 12	Dick Bailey W. ko 3	London
Sep 26	Curley Watson D. 6	London
Oct 17	Gunner Mills W. ko 4	London
Nov 30	Alf Hewitt L. 12	London
Dec 12	Stoker Potter W. ko 2	London
Dec 19	Seaman Brewer W. 6	London

1909

Jan 20	Seaman Broadbent W. 6	London
Feb 27	Curley Watson W. 6	London
Mar 22	Fred Wood W. 4	London
Apr 3	Jack Costello W. 6	London
May 8	Seaman Brewer W. 6	London
Jun 14	Blink McClusky W. 6	N.S.C.

Jul 31	Curley Watson D. 6	London
Nov 29	Jim Sullivan L. 9	N.S.C.
Dec 11	Bill Curzon W. 6	Shoreditch
	1910	
Jan 24	George Gunther L. 4	London
Apr 4	Pat Breslin W. 15	Glasgow
Apr 9	Young Johnson W. 6	London
Apr 23	Bomb. Davis W. 6	London
May 22	Bomb. Davis W. ko 1	London
	(Record Incomplete)	

JEM LAXTON

Born 26th October, 1850.   St. Luke's, London.

	Undated Contests	
	Samuel Blakelock D. 6	
	Tom Pickard Won	
	Bill Kennedy Won	
	Bob Puryer Won	
	Dan Feathers Won	
	"Soldier" W. Robinson Won	
	"Soldier" W. Robinson Won	
	Dave Cable W. 3	
	1874	
Sep 9	J. Flaherty L. 4	London
	1875	
Feb 16	Bill Richardson W. 4	London
Feb 16	Tom Hawkins W. 3	London
Feb 16	Punch Dowsett L. 3	London
(Final of 9st. 7lb. Competition)		
Dec 28	Bill Green W. 3	Shoreditch
	1876	
Jan 11	George Callow W. f. 3 (Silver Cup)	Shoreditch
Mar 13	W. Fletcher W. 3	Islington
Mar 18	Tom Hooker W. 3	Islington
Mar 18	Bob Habbijam L. 3	Islington
(Final of World 140lb. Championship Competition)		
Mar 27	Bob Habbijam W. 3 (Silver Cup)	Rotherhithe
(Final of Lightweight Competition)		
	1877	
Mar 24	Young Donnelly Won	Sadler's Wells
Mar 30	Bill Green Won	Sadler's Wells
Mar 30	"Soldier" W. Robinson L. ko 3	Sadler's Wells
(Final of 10st. Championship Competition)		

Dec 26	Challenged World at 8st. 4lb.	
	1880	
Dec 5	Tommy Orange L. ret. 3 (118-126)	London
Dec 17	Presented with Champion Bantamweight Silver Belt	
	("Having held title for over three years")	
	1882	
Mar 8	Harry Mead W. 3	Shoreditch
Mar —	Jem Gleeson W. 3	Shoreditch
Mar —	James Steadman W. 4	Shoreditch
(Final of 9st. Competition)		
	1883	
Mar 16	Harry Mead L. 3	Shoreditch
Jul 31	H. Solomons W. 3	London
(Final of 8st. 10lb. Championship Competition)		
Aug 6	Jem Hill L. 3 (112½-126)	London
—	Defeated "Soldier" W. Robinson & others to win Gold	
	Medal Competition. "The Britannia", London	
	1898	
Apr —	Pudsey Sullivan L. 3	London

JACK MALONEY

Born 1876. Westminster, London.

Undated Contests	
Alf Onslow W. 6	
George Robert W. ko 1	
Charlie Glover W. 8	Kennington
Bill Bolton W. ko 2	
Nobby Procter W. 6	
Bill Langford W. 6	
Jim Williams D. 4	
John O'Brien W. 8	
Jack Kivell W. ko 1	
Jack Kivell W. 2	
Joe Pocknell W. 6	Bill Natty's
Tom Pearson W. 4	
Jem Harding L. 5	
Joe Bennett W. 6	
Pocket Knifton Won	London
Sailor Richardson W. pts.	
Ernest Brady L. 7	
Herbert Rix L. f. 7	N.S.C.
Tom Hall L. 2	

1891
Alf Onslow Lost
1893

Oct 31	Harry Munroe W. 9	London
(English 6st. 8lb. Title)		
	1894	
Jan 8	Jack Nixon W. ret. 2	London
Feb 1	Harry Munroe W. 6	London
(English 6st. 10lb. Title)		
Mar 8	Joe Bennett W. ko 12	London
(English 6st. 10lb. Title)		
Nov —	W. Robson Lost	Eden Theatre
	1895	
Feb 6	Jim Williams Lost	—
Mar 18	Ernest Brady W. 20	Newcastle
May 13	Ernest Brady W. 20	Newcastle
Jun 3	Charlie Gledhill W. 20	Newcastle
(English 6st. 10lb. Title)		
	1896	
Jan 28	Ted Beach L. f. 12	Kennington
(English 7st. Title)		
Mar 30	Harry McDermott L. 20	Jarrow
(English 7st. Title)		
Apr —	Jim Goodson Lost	—
	1897	
May 10	Jack Guyon W. 3	N.S.C.
May 10	C. Shankster W. 3	N.S.C.
May 10	Wag Hampton W. 3	N.S.C.
	1898	
Nov 16	Tom Hall L. 8	Lambeth
	1899	
May 3	Harry Connell W. 6	Woolwich

DENVER ED MARTIN

Born 1877.

Undated Contests
Mike Queenan W. ko 2
Tom King W. ko 6
Bob Clayton W. ko 2
Mexican Pete W. ko 14
Bob Armstrong W. 12
Charlie Stevens W. 14

	Walter Johnson W. ko 7	
	John Klondyke W. ko 5	
	Bob Armstrong W. ko 5	
	Tom Carey W. ko 2	
	Frank Scully W. ko 1	
	Jim Galvin W. ko 1	
	Yank Kenny W. ko 1	
	Earle Thompson W. ko 1	
	Bud Jackson W. ko 3	
	Ike Hayes W. ko 2	
	Fred Russell W. 10	
	Hank Griffin W. ko 7	
	Frank Childs W. ko 6	
(Coloured Heavyweight Championship of World)		
	Bob Armstrong D. 6	
	1902	
Jun 25	John Sandy Ferguson W. ko 5	N.S.C.
(English Heavyweight Title)		
Jul 25	Bob Armstrong W. 15	Crystal Palace
(English Heavyweight Title)		
Aug 16	Frank Craig W. rsf 3	Newcastle
Aug 20	Frank Craig W. ko 4	Newcastle
	1903	
Feb 3	Jack Johnson L. 20	Los Angeles
(Coloured Heavyweight Championship of World)		
Sep 15	Sam McVea L. ko 1	Los Angeles
	1904	
Aug 13	Sam McVea W. ko 10	Los Angeles
Oct 18	Jack Johnson L. ko 2	Los Angeles
	1909	
—	Gunboat Smith nd 6	—

MIKE 'CHAPPIE' MORAN

Born 12th December, 1868.   Birmingham, England.

Died 3rd April, 1896.

	1887-1888	
	Tom Fisher W. 93m.	London
	Patsy Sheehan L. pts	London
	Tom Varley W. 9	Birmingham
	Fred Brown W. 4	London
	Billy Plimmer L. 3	
	Billy Plimmer L. 8	

	1889	
	D. O'Brien Lost	
	Jim Watson W. 4	Jersey City
	Bill Hensail W. 3	Knicker Bocker Gardens
	Jack Lynch W. 4	Philadelphia
	Jim Watson W. 6	Paterson
May 21	Frank Donovan W. ko 14	Staten Isle
(American Bantamweight Title)		
Jun —	Tommy Kelly L. 4	Hoboken
(World Bantamweight Title)		
Jun 5	Tommy Kelly W. 10	Greenpoint
(World Bantamweight Title)		
Jul 29	Peter Sherry W. 4	Jersey City
	1890	
Jan 31	Tommy Kelly L. ko 10 (105lb.)	Easton, Pa.
(Advertised as American Bantamweight Title)		
—	Sid Phillips L. 20	—
—	Sid Phillips L. 4	N.S.C.
Dec 22	Patsy Sheehan W. 8	London
	1891	
Jun 10	Patsy Sheehan W. 20	N.S.C.
—	George Smith W. 6	Birmingham
	1892	
Feb —	Jack Finlay W. ko 4	New York
Feb 27	Frank Donovan W. ko 5	Manhatton
Apr 5	Eddie Avery D. 10 (105lb.)	Williamsburg
(American Bantamweight Title)		
	1893	
Dec 11	George Corfield L. 20	Sheffield
(English 7st. 12lb. Title)		
	1894	
Jul 30	Tom Fitzpatrick W. 20	Sheffield
(English 7st. 9lb. Title)		

HARRY McDERMOTT

Born 1875.   South Shields.   Died 14th December, 1953.

	1894	
Nov	— Tigue W. ret. 1	Manchester
Nov	— Wood W. ko 1	Manchester
Nov	James Carlin W. ko 4	Gateshead
Nov	Billy Hughes W. ko 3	Ryhope
Nov	Sammy Francis W. 12	
	Ernest Brady W. 20	

1896

Mar 30	Jack Maloney W. 20	Jarrow
(English 7st. Title)		
Oct 19	Ted Beach W. 15	Gateshead
(English 7st. 6lb. Title)		
Dec 14	James Freeman W. ko 4	Holloway
(English 7st. 8lb. Title)		
—	Charles Taylor W. 4	Newcastle

1897

?? —	Harry Slough L. 1 (Result/fight doubtful)	—
(English 7st. 6lb. Title)		
Mar 29	Mike Small W. ko 10	Gateshead
Jun 2	Harry Brodigan W. f. 8	Gateshead
Nov 22	Ernest Brady W. ko 17	Gateshead
(English 7st. 6lb. Title)		

1898

Feb 25	Charlie Taylor W. rsf 7	Sheffield
(English 7st. 6lb. Title)		
Mar 1	George Beach L. ko 5	Sheffield
(English 7st. 6lb. Title)		
Mar 22	Jack Guyon W. ko 7	Gateshead

1899

Apr 1	Charlie Exall W. ko 14	Gateshead
(English 7st. 4lb. Title) (Exall 3lb. Overweight)		

1900

Apr 16	Charlie Exall W. 12	Newcastle
Apr 20	Kid Veitch W. rsf 8	Newcastle
(Final of 7st. 10lb. Championship Competition)		

1901

Jul 22	Charlie Exhall W. 20	Gateshead
(English 7st. 10lb. Title)		

1902

Sep 27	Charlie Exall L. ret. 8	Newcastle
(Match made at 7st. 8lb. 2-minute rounds)		
Oct 2	Tibby Watson W. rsf 8	Newcastle
(World 7st. 10lb. Paperweight Title)		
Nov 15	Jim Kenrick W. 15	Newcastle
(World & English Paperweight Titles)		
Dec ?	Charlie Exall L. ko 8	Newcastle
(World & English Paperweight Titles)		
—	Andrew Wood W. 10	—

1903

Jan 31	Dave Job L. ko 4	Newcastle
Oct 24	Jack Player W. ret. 6	Newcastle
Nov 14	Jack Fitzpatrick W. ko 3	Newcastle

Dec 26	Johnny Hughes W. rsf 3	Newcastle
	1904	
Feb 6	Jack Guyon W. rsf 7	Newcastle
Jul 11	Digger Stanley L. ko 6	Newcastle
Oct 17	Digger Stanley L. ko 19	Newcastle
Nov 26	Jack Christian W. rsf 1	Newcastle
	1908	
Feb 10	Albert Cocksedge Lost	Leicester
	1909	
Oct —	Curley Osborne Won	Newcastle
Dec 1	Curley Osborne W. ko 6	Newcastle
	1910	
Jan 31	Joe Percival W. 20	Newcastle
(English 7st. 6lb. Title)		
Apr 7	Albert Cocksedge L. 20	Newcastle
(English 7st. 12lb. Title)		
Jun 13	Joe Shears W. 20	Newcastle
Oct 10	Joe Wilson L. ko 13	Newcastle
—	Joe Fox L. 15	—
	1911	
Jan 9	Joe Fox L. 15	Leeds
Feb 13	Louis Ruddick L. 20	Newcastle
Mar 20	Charlie Exhall L. 15	South Shields
May 27	Jack McGurk D.	Jarrow
	1912	
Jan 6	Charlie Cooper L. ko 3	South Shields

CHARLIE McKEEVER

Born 19th November, 1873.   Slatington, Pa.

	1894	
Jul 27	Owen Ziegler L. ko 3	Atlantic City
	Jack Daly D. 6	
	Tom Farrell W. 2	
	Jimmy Mitchell W. 3	
	Billy Darragh W. 4	
	Jack McAuliffe D. 8	
	Bull McCarthy D. 4	
Dec 20	Stanton Abbott W. 6	Philadelphia
Dec 22	Owen Ziegler Exh. 4	Philadelphia
	Tom Moriarty D. 6	
	1895	
	Jack Hanley W. ko 3	

Horace Leeds L. ko 4
Jack Everhardt Drew
Arthur Valentine W. ko 17
1896

Jan 15	Owen Ziegler nd 6	Philadelphia
Apr 13	Young Griffo W. 20	Maspeth
Jul 20	Kid Lavigne nd 4	New York
	Billy McCarthy W. 6	
	Charley Johnson W. 6	
	George Green Lost	

1897

Feb 1	Owen Ziegler nd 6	Philadelphia
—	Tom Williams Won	—
Mar 8	Kid Lavigne nd 6	Philadelphia
Dec 13	Matty Matthews D. 15	Athens, Pa.

1898

Apr 12	Matty Matthews W. 20	Cleveland
—	Frank McConnell L. 4	—
Oct 7	Myst. Billy Smith L. 25	New York

(World Welterweight Title)

1899

Feb 7	Rube Ferns W. 6	Chicago
Jun 26	Owen Ziegler W. 8	Coney Isle
Jun 30	Myst. Billy Smith D. 20	New York

(World Welterweight Title)

Oct —	Myst. Billy Smith nd 6	Philadelphia
Nov 8	Myst. Billy Smith L. 20	New York
—	Charlie Burns Drew	—

1900

—	Jimmy Handler L. f.	—
—	Charlie Burns W. 20	—
Oct 15	Dido Plumb W. 15	N.S.C.

(English Middleweight Title)

—	Jack Bennett (Failed to stop) 15

1901

Sep —	Jack Palmer n/c 2	Newcastle
Dec 9	Jack Palmer W. 12	Newcastle

(English Middleweight Title)

1902

Jan 27	Phil. Jack O'Brien L. f. 3	London

(English Middleweight Title)

HARRY NICKLESS

Born 1866.   Kew, Surrey.   Died 23rd October, 1899.

	Connie Collins W. 4	"Hop & Malt"
	1889	
Jun —	Jem Sullivan W. 12	Pelican Club
	George Baxter Won	Newmarket
	Ted Fenton Won	Pelican Club
	Barney Sheppard	
Aug —	Alf Suffolk W. 13	South London
	Jem Townsend L. pts.	
	Jem Townsend W. 14	"Hop & Malt"
Oct 14	Jem Townsend W. 6	London
	1891	
Mar 11	Johnny Robinson W. ko 6	Ormonde Club
(English 10st. 4lb. Title)		
—	Harry Kelly W. ko 1	N.S.C.
Jun ?	Bill Hatcher W. ko 9	Bolinsbroke Club
(English 10st. Title)		
	1894	
Feb 12	Barclay Perkins Exh. 3	London
Feb 19	Dick Chandler D. 3	Manchester
May 4	Dick Burge L. ko 28	London
(English 10st. Title)		

JOHN O'BRIEN

Born 20th December, 1867.   Cardiff.

	Jem Driscoll W. 6	Cardiff
	Peter Burns W. 3	Cardiff
	"Shonnie" W. 19m. (Knuckles) (£100)	—
(Welsh Championship)		
	Felix Scott W. 3	Liverpool
	1890	
Nov 25	Ted Bryant L. 1 (27sec.)	Soho
	1891	
Mar 7	Ted White W. ko 9 (£90)	Haymarket
May 27	Alf Ball W. 7 (£120)	Haymarket
Dec 21	Alf Mitchell W. 8 (11st. 4lb.) (£300)	N.S.C.
(English Middleweight Title)		
	1894	
Apr 23	David St. John W. ko 5 (£150)	N.S.C.

Oct 8	Frank Craig L. ko 2	N.S.C.

(English Middleweight Title)
1895

Apr 13	Frank Craig L. ko 1	London

HARRY OVERTON

1889

Feb	Harry Mead Lost	London

1890

Aug 22	Billy Reader W. ko 13	Walworth

(English 9st. Title)
1891

May 25	Bill Whalley W. 7	N.S.C.
Nov 23	Billy Reader L. ko 4	N.S.C.

(English 9st. Title)
1892

Feb 29	Stanton Abbott L. 12	N.S.C.

1893

May 8	Arthur Valentine L. 14	N.S.C.

1894

Oct 1	Tom Woolley W. 12	Birmingham

DIDO PLUMB

Born 1874. London.	Died 1916.

1889

Mar 12	Bill Husband L. 3	London
	Jem Adds Won	
	Bill Hill Won	

1893

Dec 14	Kit Marney W. 12	London

1894

Jan 15	Charles 'Toff' Wall Exh. 3	Shoreditch

1895

Oct 14	Jack Lewis W. 1	N.S.C.
Nov 26	Jerry Driscoll W. ko 4	N.S.C.

1896

Feb 5	Myst. Billy Smith Exh. 3	N.S.C.
Jun 1	Ted White L. rsf 16	N.S.C.

(English Middleweight Title)
1897

Apr 26	Fred Morris W. 10	N.S.C.

J

1898
Feb 25	Jem Richardson Won	Birmingham
Feb 25	Anthony Diamond L. 12	Birmingham

(Final of 11st. Championship Competition)

May 23	Aust. Billy Edwards W. ko 4	N.S.C.

1899
May 2	Bill Hefferman Won	N.S.C.

1900
Mar 19	Jem Ryan W. rsf 8 (154lb.)	N.S.C.

(English Middleweight Title)

Oct 15	Charlie McKeever L. 15	N.S.C.

(English Middleweight Title)

1901
Aug 19	Phil. Jack O'Brien L. ko 6	Newcastle

(English Middleweight Title)

1902
Dec 15	Charlie Wilson D. 8	Wonderland

1910
Mar 3	Frank Craig D. 6	London

TED PRITCHARD

Born 1866.   Lambeth   Died 20th November, 1903.

1887

Won two competitions in South London

	George Ashley W. ko 2	Plumstead
	Jack Casey W. ko 2	Plumstead
Dec —	Dave Galvin W. ko 3	Wood Green
Dec —	Dick Leary W. ko 2	Wood Green
Dec —	Dave Burke W. 4	Wood Green

(Final of Frank Hynde's 10st. 2lb. Competition)

1889
Feb 19	Jim Hayes W. rsf 4 (144lb.)		Lambeth
Jun 6	Alec Burns W. ko 2	(148lb.)	Lambeth

1890
—	Alf Mitchell W. ko 4 (154lb.)	Soho

1891
Mar 12	Jack Burke W. ko 3 (154lb.)	Holloway

(English Middleweight Title)

Jul 27	Jem Smith W. ko 3	New Cross

(English Heavyweight Title)

	1892	
—	Jem Hall D. 6	N.S.C.
Aug 20	Jem Hall L. ko 4 (158lb.)	N.S.C.
(English Middleweight Title)		
	1894	
Nov 26	Dick Burge W. ko 2	London
(English Middleweight Title)		
Dec 17	Frank Craig L. ko 1 (158lb.)	Holborn
(English Middleweight Title)		
	1895	
May 10	Jem Smith L. ko 2 (160-182)	Holborn
(English Heavyweight Title)		

WILLIAM READER

Fulham

	1887	
Dec	Dave Burke Won	
	1888	
May	Edwin Davies Won	Haymarket
May	Dido Hopkins Won	Haymarket
May 14	Dave Burke W. 10	Haymarket
(Final of 9st. Championship Competition)		
	1889	
Feb 23	Stanton Abbott Lost	—
Apr 23	Fred Johnson W. 3	Wood Green
Apr 25	Bill Baxter L. 3	Wood Green
	1890	
Aug 22	Harry Overton L. ko 13	Ormonde Club
(English 9st. Title)		
Oct 14	Samuel Blakelock W. 12	London
	1891	
Apr 27	Bill Baxter W. ko 16	N.S.C.
(English 9st. Title)		
Nov 23	Harry Overton W. ko 4	N.S.C.
(English 9st. Title)		
	1892	
Dec 19	Harry Spurden L. 20	N.S.C.
(English 9st. Title)		

ALEC ROBERTS

Born 1859.   London.   Died 9th November, 1899.

1884
Arthur Cooper Won   London
Won 11st. Competition   Hoxton
Pat Condon W. 33r. 88m. (Knuckles) (£25 Purse)   Downham
1885
George Caseley Won   London
Tom Smith Won   —
Bill Goode Won   London
Ted Burchell Won   London
Jem Kendrick L. 6   —
1886
Connie Collins W. 29m. (Knuckles)   Isle of Sovereigns
Pat Condon W. 6   —
1887
Jan 19   Jack Passfield Won   Marylebone
Jan 19   Josh Alexander Won   Marylebone
Jan19   Jack Donoghue Won   Marylebone
(Final of Bob Habbijam's 10st. 8lb. Championship Competition)
Oct 17   Alec Burns D. 12   London
1888
Jan 25   Jack Edmonds Won   Marylebone
Jan 25   Arthur Cooper Won   Marylebone
(Final of Bob Habbijam's 10st 8lb. Championship Competition)
Arthur Bobbett W. 6   —
Feb 15   Alec Burns W. 12 (146-148)   London
May 19   Jem Hayes W. 63r. 112m. (Knuckles)   London District
Sep 24   Arthur Bobbett D. 53r. 211m.   Lambeth
(English 10st. 7lb. Title)
—   Arthur Bobbett W. 6   —
—   Pat Condon D. 12   London

JACK ROBERTS

Born 11th November, 1873.   Broadstairs, Kent.

Undated Contests
Joe Broad W. pts. 4
Tom Wren W. pts. 4
Ted White W. pts. 4
Jack Hardcastle W. rsf 2

	Joe Wooton W. pts. 4	
	Jewey Cooke W. pts. 4	
	Frank Griggs W. pts. 4	
	Jack McGee W. pts. 6	
	Jem Barry L. pts. 6	
	Alf Green W. pts. 10	
	Frank Guess Won	
	Tom Turner W. pts. 6	
	1894	
Nov 3	Jack Stanley W. ko 2	London
	1896	
	Frank Lowry W. pts. 10	N.S.C.
Mar 12	Tom Phillips W. 8	N.S.C.
Apr 27	Jem Barry W. 10	N.S.C.
	Jack Goldswain L. 3	—
	Jem Barry W. rsf 7	N.S.C.
	Bill Brierley W. ko 7	N.S.C.
	Nat Smith W. ret. 2	N.S.C.
Oct 26	Charlie Meacock L. pts. 11	N.S.C.
	Nat Smith W. 20	N.S.C.
Nov 23	Bill Wood W. 6	N.S.C.
Dec 14	Bill Wood W. 10	N.S.C.
	1897	
Jan 18	Charlie Meacock L. ko 5	N.S.C.
Mar —	Bill Eastwick L. 6	Holloway
Apr 26	Alf Green W. 6	N.S.C.
May 17	Alf Green W. 10	N.S.C.
—	Bill Wood L. ko 2	N.S.C.
Oct 18	Ted Marlow W. 5	N.S.C.
Nov 22	Bill Eyles W. 6	Bethnal Green
Dec 3	Bill Wood W. 6	London
Dec 9	Bill Wood W. 10	Bethnal Green
	1898	
Jan 10	Bill Brierley W. rsf 7	N.S.C.
Jan 20	Harry Benson L. 6	Bethnal Green
Feb 1	Ted Ware L. ko 3	Bethnal Green
Feb 17	Jerry Donoghue W. ko 3	London
Apr 9	Harry Benson W. 6	Bethnal Green
Apr 18	Harry Benson L. 10	Bethnal Green
May 6	Nat Smith W. 20	N.S.C.
Oct 10	Bill Wood W. ko 10	N.S.C.
	1899	
Feb 27	Frank Guess W. 20	N.S.C.
Mar 6	Bill Chester W. 6	N.S.C.

Oct 23	Jack Goldswain L. ko 6	N.S.C.
Dec 12	Tom Ireland L. ret. 5	N.S.C.
	1901	
Jan 21	Will Curley W. ko 7	N.S.C.
(English 9st. Title)		
Apr 22	Billy Smith W. ko 8	N.S.C.
(English Featherweight Title)		
	1902	
Feb 3	Will Curley L. ko 3	Newcastle
(English 9st. Title)		
Oct 20	Ben Jordan L. ko 5	N.S.C.
(English Featherweight Title)		
	1903	
Mar 30	Dick Lee L. ret. 9	London
Aug 1	George Procter L. pts. 6	London
Oct 17	George Justice W. pts. 20	Newcastle
Dec 14	George Proctor W. pts. 6	N.S.C.
	1904	
Mar 21	Young Joseph W. ko 7	N.S.C.
Apr 18	Johnny Summers D. 6	London
May 16	Young Joseph W. 10	N.S.C.
Jun 18	Young Joseph L. 6	London
Aug 26	George Justice D. 15	London
Oct 31	Spike Robson L. ko 10	N.S.C.
Dec 8	Boss Edwards L. 15	London
	1905	
Feb 13	Wally Morgan L. 15	N.S.C.
Apr 17	Marcel Mois W. ko 1	N.S.C.
May 16	Johnny Summers D. 6	London
Jul 1	Kid Lavigne L. ko 6	Paris
Aug 5	Bob White W. ko 6	West Hartlepool
Oct 23	Will Cameron W. rsf 2	N.S.C.
Dec 4	Allan Littlefield L. 6	N.S.C.
Dec 16	Will Cameron W. ko 5	Cardiff
	1906	
Jan 25	Ted Ward W. 6	Marylebone
Feb 13	Wally Morgan L. 15	N.S.C.
Feb 26	Jim Driscoll L. rsf 7	N.S.C.
Mar 10	Alf Wood L. 6	London
May 15	Ted Ward L. 6	London
May 29	Ted Ward L. 6	London
Oct 18	Alf Vango L. rsf 4	N.S.C.
Nov 19	Sam Johnson L. ret. 4	Newcastle
Dec 19	Alf Wood L. 6	London

	1907	
Feb 4	Young Joseph L. 10	Colchester
Feb 25	Alf Wood W. 6	Westminster
Mar 18	Young Tom Sharkey L. 6	N.S.C.
Nov 11	Harry Brown L. ret. 12	Plymouth
Nov 27	Stoker Rogers L. 10	Plymouth
	1908	
Jan 1	Jim Driscoll L. rsf 2	Aberdare
	1909	
Jan 25	Dick Curtis W. 4	Hammersmith
Feb 1	Dick Dean W. 4	Putney
Feb 8	Alf Clarke L. ret. 3	Walworth
Jul 16	Alf Wood L. 4	Charing Cross
Dec 27	Sgt. Rust W. 6	Holborn
	1910	
Mar 7	Sid Hunt W. 6	Holborn
Jul 23	Bill Wood W. 6	Clapton

W. ROBINSON
'Soldier'

Born 1854.   Clerkenwell.

	Undated Contests	
	Hinton Won (Gold Medal)	Britannia Tavern, London
	Williams Won (Silver Cup)	—
	1876	
Mar 13	Bob Puryer W. 3	Islington
Apr	Lumpy Hughes W. 3	London
Apr	Alf Patten W. 3	London
Apr	Bob Habbijam W. 3 (Silver Cup)	London
	1877	
Mar 24	Bill Hooker Won	Sadler's Wells
Mar 30	— Ward Won	Sadler's Wells
Mar 30	Jim Laxton W. ko 3	Sadler's Wells
(Final of 10st. Championship Competition)		
	1878	
Sep 18	T. Stockley W. 16r. 63m. (£20)	Shadwell

JACK SCALES

Born 20th September, 1874.

	1898-1899	
	Starlight W. 5	N.S.C.

	J. J. Mottram W. 3	N.S.C.
	Fred Greenbock W. 2	
	Arthur Morris W. 2	
	Cpl. McFadden W. 1	
	Tom Mack W. 1	
	1899	
Feb 9	Edgar Beard W. rsf 1	Wonderland
—	Jack Broderick W. 2	London
(Final of Heavyweight Championship Competition)		
Nov 14	Tom Lees W. ko 2	Marylebone
	1900	
Feb 9	Dick Burge L. ko 1	London
Mar —	Pat Daley L. 3	Wonderland
Sep 30	George Gardiner L. f. 4	N.S.C.
Oct 13	Stonnet Dixon W. 7	—
	1901	
Jan 7	Cloggy Saunders W. 2	London
Mar 16	Jack Walsh W. ko 2	London
Apr 22	Harry Neumier L. 5	London
Aug 3	Phil. Jack O'Brien L. 6	Newcastle
Sep 23	Jack Palmer W. 11	Newcastle
Nov 7	Phil. Jack O'Brien L. ko 1	Liverpool
Dec 2	Kid McCoy L. ko 1	London
	1902	
Jan 4	Slouch Dixon W. 6	London
Jan 13	Harry Neumier W. 6	London
Jun 25	Ben Taylor W. ko 10	London
(Coronation Heavyweight Championship Belt)		
Oct 13	Slouch Dixon W. ko 7	N.S.C.
(English Heavyweight Title)		
Nov 8	Charlie Wilson L. ko 3	London
(English Heavyweight Title)		
	1904	
Jul 23	Jack Kingsland W. 6	London
Aug 13	Andrew Jeptha W. 6	London
Oct 1	Jack Kingsland W. 6	London
Oct 26	Young Peter Jackson L. ko 4	Newcastle
Dec 3	Ben Taylor W. 6	London
Dec 15	Mike Shallow D. 10	Newport
(Advertised as English Heavyweight Title)		
Dec 31	Pte. Casling W. ko 4	London

	1905	
Feb 25	Bomb. Kibbler W. 3	Portsmouth
Apr 1	Charlie Knock L. 6	London
	1906	
Dec 29	Fred Higgins W. ko 2	London
	1907	
Jan 12	Mike Crawley W. 6	London
Apr 29	Frank Craig L. 6	London
May 11	Charlie Knock L. 6	London
Jun 15	Herbert Hall W. 4	London
Jul 13	Frank Craig W. 6	London
Aug 3	Herbert Hall W. 2	London
Oct 5	Charlie Allum W. 6	London
Oct 19	Charlie Key W. 3	London
Oct 28	Iron Hague D. 6	Sheffield
Nov 9	Ben Taylor W. 6	London
Dec 28	Sam McVea L. 2	Paris
	1908	
Mar 5	Steve Smith L. 10	London
Apr 25	Charlie Wilson L. 5	Paris
May 11	Iron Hague L. ko 2	Sheffield
Jun 13	Jewey Smith W. 6	London
Aug 29	Jewey Smith W. 6	London
Nov 14	Jewey Smith L. 6	London
Nov 30	Harry Shearing W. ko 4	London
Dec 5	Seaman McDonald W. 3	London
	1909	
Jan 2	Jewey Smith L. 8	London
Jan 16	Bill Johnson W. 2	London
Feb 20	Harry Barrett D. 6	London
Mar 6	Mike Crawley W. 6	London
Mar 20	Harry Shearing L. 3	London
May 1	Joe Jeanette L. ko 1	Paris
Oct 23	Jewey Smith L. 5	London
Dec 20	Dan Voyles L. 6	N.S.C.
	1910	
Jan 24	Herbert Hall L. 6	London
Oct 1	Cpl. Brown L. ko 4	—
	1911	
Mar ?	P.O. Curran L. ko 4	Plymouth
(British Heavyweight Title)		

138

WILLIAM SHERiFF
'The Prussian'

Born 1st August, 1847.   Leicester.   Died 4th June, 1893.

Joe Barrows W. 30m.
Jack Marshall W. 40m.
Fred Haughton W. 50m.
George Haughton W. 210m.
Jack Haughton W. 34m.
— Davis Drew
1880
Dec 17   Denny Harrington W. 11r. 40m. (Police) (152-149)   Lapworth
(World & English Middleweight Titles)
1883
Jan 13   Alf Greenfield Exh. 3   Birmingham
Oct 2   Charlie Mitchell D. 7 (175-150)   Flushing
1884
Jan 30   G. W. Sawdry Won   Toledo
Apr 10   John Welch D. 76r. 303m. (175-160)   Philadelphia
Apr 18   Mike Cleary L. ko 1 (174-164)   New York
—   Dominick McCaffrey L. pts.   Pittsburgh
May 8   Jake Kilrain L. 3 (Police)   Boston

MIKE SMALL

Born 1873.   London.

Undated Contests
Wag Lansdowne W. 8
Wag Lansdowne W. 20
Bill Burley W. 8
Jack Hicks W. 13
George Murray W. 8
George Murray W. 10
George Murray W. 5
Jack Sheehan W. 6
Bill Rose W. 3
Ted Newell W. 7
Charley Wright W. 10
Dick Cuddings W. 6
Dick Cuddings W. 6
Fred Harvey W. 5
Dol Hunt W. 3

Bill Thorne D. 24
Bill Thorne D. 12
Bill Thorne L. 12
Jack Hutchings W. 6
Charley Wright W. 3
Jack Sheehan W. 4
Ernie Pickard W. 6
Ernie Pickard W. 6
Ernie Pickard W. 6
Alf Green W. 6   Croydon
Fred Sullivan W. 6   Kennington
Jack Rose W. 5
Ted Hall W. 2   Norfolk
Bert Smith W. 4
George Miller W. 8
Sid Phillips Drew
Sid Phillips D. 6
Con Rous W. ko 5
Joe Berry W. 4
Bill Moore L. 24
Bill Moore Drew
Jack Russell W. 12
Jack Russell W. 12
Dick Cozens W. 6
Dick Cozens W. 6
Jem Knowles L. 20
— Leatherwell W. 5
Ted Yarnell W. 10
Lall Hunt W. 5
Bill Moore L. 8
Bill Moore L. 8
Bill Moore L. 6
Bill Moore L. 6
1890
Bill Corbett Won
1892?
Bill Mortimer W. 5
(English 7st. 4lb. Title)
1893
May 29   Pedler Palmer L. 6   N.S.C.
Oct 10   Harry Brown W. 3   Wolverhampton
(English 7st. 4lb. Title)
1894
Feb 12   George Murray W. 6   Goodwin Gym.

Dec 3	Ernie Pickard W. rsf 18	N.S.C.
(English 7st. 4lb. Title)		
	1895	
Feb 25	Jack Pearson L. 20	N.S.C.
(English 7st. 4lb. Title)		
	1896	
Mar 2	Joe Gates W. 5	N.S.C.
Oct —	Jack Pearson L. 20	N.S.C.
(English 7st. 4lb. Title)		
Nov 30	Walter Croot L. 11	N.S.C.
(English 7st. 4lb. Title)		
	1897	
—	Charlie Simpson W. 20	—
Mar 29	Harry McDermott L. ko 10	Gateshead
Aug 2	Bob Bailey W. ko 7	Bethnal Green
(English 7st. 6lb. Title)		
	1898	
Jan 31	Ernest Brady W. ko 3	Gateshead
Sep 10	Jem Lee L. ko 4	Dublin

HARRY SPURDEN

Born 6th February, 1869.   Cambridge.

	Undated Contests	
	Darkey Barton L. 4	London
	Darkey Barton W. 6	—
	Darkey Barton W. 8	—
	Fred Suckling W. 6	Shoreditch
	Fred Suckling W. 6	Shoreditch
	Andrew Jacobs W. ko 12	Battersea
	Darkey Barton W. 6	Newmarket
	Harry Brown W. 12	Westgate-on-Sea
	Tom Jefford Won	Kennington
	Ginger Elmer W. 4	Clapham
	Peter Connor W. 6	London
	1890?	
	Bill Corbett W. f. 39r. 210m.	Kennington
(English Featherweight Title?)		
Sep 15	Bill Corbett W. 26r. 99m.	Lambeth
(English Featherweight Title?)		
	1891	
Dec 19	Stanton Abbott L. pts. 4	Kennington
(Final of 9st. Championship Competition)		

	1892	
Feb 1	Tom Jeffords W. ret. 6	N.S.C.
Dec 19	Billy Reader W. 20	N.S.C.
(English 9st. Title)		
	1893	
Dec 6	Arthur Callan W. 11	London
	1894	
Jun 27	Darkey Barton W. 22	N.S.C.
(English 9st. Title)		
—	Darkey Barton D. 10	—
—	Darkey Barton Exh. 3	—
	1895	
Feb 6	Jack Fitzpatrick L. ko 7	Clapham
(English 9st. Title)		
	1897	
Feb 8	Tom Ireland L. 10	N.S.C.
	1898	
Feb 17	Fred Johnson W. 3	London
Apr 18	George Cunningham L. rsf 3	Bethnal Green
(Final of 9st. Championship Competition)		
—	Dave Smith W. ret. 6	Bethnal Green
	1900	
Feb 28	Harry Chamberlain L. 10	Wonderland
Mar 18	Harry Benson L. ko 4	Wonderland
	1901	
Jan 5	Fred Johnson W. ko 2	—

JEM STEVENS

Born 9th February, 1868.

Undated Contests	
Young Hooker W. 8	
J. Green W. 2	
Jack Russell W. 6	
Johnny Onslow W. 1	
Ted Mortimer W. 1	
Charles Tilley L. 3	Goodwin Club
Ponk Andrews W. 8	
— Portley L. 6	
Ike Hore W. 6	
Jack Fitzgibbons W. 4	
Tommy Marin W. 12	

1885?

	Art Levy W. 6	—
(English 6st. Title)		
	1890	
Dec —	Tom De Groat W. 5	London
(English 7st. 4lb. Title)		
	1891	
Jan 30	Herbert Tarrant W. 12	London
May 31	Billy Plimmer L. ret. 15	London
(English 8st. Title)		
Oct 13	Won 8st. Competition	N.S.C.
	1892	
Dec 21	Harry Webster W. 10	N.S.C.
	1893	
Jan 16	Bill Corbett W. 20	N.S.C.
Feb 13	James Howe W. 20	Gateshead
May 8	John Johnson L. 18	Newcastle

BILL STONELAKE

Clerkenwell, London.

	Undated Contests	
	Jim Williams W. 6	
	Bill Lampshire Lost	
	Bill Lampshire Lost	
	Bill Lampshire Lost	
	Harry Paul L. ko 8	Wonderland
	Tom Rippington W. pts.	
	Harry Churchill L. 4	
	George Proctor L. 6	
	Dan Cripps L. 6	
	1895	
Sep 28	Bill Exall W. ko 1	London
	1897	
Mar 17	Won 7st. Competition	Holloway
Dec 1	Charles Broadbent W. ko 2	London
	1898	
Feb 26	Charlie Exall W. 6	London
Mar 14	Bill Hutchinson L. rsf 9	N.S.C.
Mar —	Dave Morbin L. ko 3	London
Apr 6	Bill Norton Won	Bethnal Green

Nov 4	Bill Richardson L. rsf 3	N.S.C.
	1900	
Jan 17	Bill Hullett W. ret. 3	Woolwich
	1901	
Jan 6	Dick Parkes W. ko 3	Wonderland
(Final of 8st. 4lb. Championship Competition)		
—	Alf Greer L. ko 4	Wonderland
	1902	
Jun 26	Alf Payne W. 4	New Adelphi Club
(Coronation 8st. 6lb. Championship Belt)		

ANDREW TOKELL

Born 1st March, 1878.   Jarrow-on-Tyne.

	Undated Contests	
	Cocklegene W. 6	
	Cummings W. 4	
	Dennis W. ko 7	
	Lord W. ko	Germany
	Daley W. 2	
	Buckerlyne W. 2	
	Bill Lampshire Won	N.S.C.
	1898	
Mar 8	William Lord W. 7	Barnsley
Apr 25	Jack Whelan W. ko 7	—
—	Bill Richards W. 12	—
Aug 22	Andrew Wood L. 20	Gateshead
Oct —	Bill Lampshire W. ko 8	Gateshead
	1900	
Oct 1	George Slark W. 9	Gateshead
	1901	
Feb 15	George Corfield W. ko 4	Newcastle
Sep 2	Bob Wilkinson W. 20	Gateshead
	1902	
Jan 20	Tom King W. ret. 8	Newcastle
Feb 13	Harry Ware W. 20	London
(English Bantamweight Title)		
May 12	Jim Williams W. f. 10	N.S.C.
(English Bantamweight Title)		
Sep 8	Harry Ware L. f. 8	London
Oct 21	Harry Paul W. ret. 11	Newcastle

1903

May 25	Joe Bowker L. 20	N.S.C.

(English Bantamweight Title)

Aug 31	Harry Ware L. f. 10	Newcastle

1904

Mar 7	Owen Moran L. 12	London
Dec 24	Frankie Neil L. 2	Wakefield

1905

Aug 24	Young Burke W. 3	Dublin

1908

Apr 30	Kid Saxby L. 15	Leeds

JACK WALKER

Paddington, London.

1894

Jan 4	Jack Fitzgibbons L. ko 3	Goode's Gym.
Feb 1	Harry Munroe W. 6	London

1896

Apr 8	Joe Barrett W. ko 12	Amberley
Oct 2	D. Murphy W. ret. 1	N.S.C.
Oct 2	Tom Snow W. 3	N.S.C.
Oct 2	Dan Dudley L. 3	N.S.C.

1897

Mar 12	A. Broadbent Won	Kennington
Mar 12	Dick Curtis Lost	Kennington
May 17	George Slark W. 6	N.S.C.
Nov 1	Johnny Thomas W. rsf. 3	N.S.C.

(English 7st. 12lb. Title)

1898

Jan 21	Alf Greer W. 6	N.S.C.
Mar 1	Jack Hare W. 2	N.S.C.
Mar 3	Dave Morbin W. rsf 6	N.S.C.
Mar —	Joe Barrett Won	Sheffield
Mar 8	George Corfield L. 10	Sheffield

(Final of 8st. Championship Competition)

May 18	G. Greaves W. ko 5	Bethnal Green
—	Charlie Exall L. 20	London

(English 7st. 10lb. Title)

1899

Apr —	Ike Cohen W. pts.	Manchester

1900

Apr —	Alf Green L. 6	Wonderland

	1901	
Dec 22	Ernie Moody W. 15	National Athletic Club
(English 7st. 12lb. Title)		
	1902	
Feb 10	Charlie Exall L. 20	London
(English 7st. 10lb. Title)		
	1903	
Mar 2	Digger Stanley L. 12	London
(English 7st. 12lb. Title)		
May 25	Owen Moran L. 15	N.S.C.
(English 8st. Title)		
Dec 14	Digger Stanley L. 15	N.S.C.
(English 8st. Title)		
	1904	
—	Owen Moran L. ko 2	—

CHARLES 'TOFF' WALL

Born 1863.   Hackney.

	Undated Contests	
	Jack Donoghue Won	Shoreditch
	Arthur Cooper Won	Shoreditch
	Jem Picton Won	Shoreditch
	Jack Partridge Won	Shoreditch
	Jack Donoghue Won	Shoreditch
	Jem Burchell Won	Shoreditch
	Tom Hill W. rsf 4 (136-126)	London
	Rough Pearson W. 77m. (Knuckles)	Chingford
	1886	
	Jem Smith Exh.	—

(Wall completely outclassed Smith, knocking him down)

	1887	
Feb —	Jack Knifton W. 3	London

(Final of Catchweight Competition)
(With the absence of Charlie Mitchell in America Wall had established himself as the best heavyweight in England although weighing only ten stone)

—	Bill Samuels W. ko 2	Cardiff
	1888	
Dec —	Ted Burchell W. 3	Westminster
Dec —	Mike Moore W. 3	Westminster
Dec —	Alf Mitchell W. 4	Westminster

1890

Feb 8	Bill Goode W. 12	Haymarket
(English Middleweight Title)		

1894

Jan 15	Dido Plumb Exh. 3	Shoreditch
Dec 3	Dido Plumb Exh. 4	Goodwin Club

1896

Feb —	Jem Smith Exh.	London

JABEZ WHITE

Born 20th October, 1873.   Birmingham.

1895

Ted Marlow W. 6	Birmingham
George Edge W. ko 3	Birmingham

1896

Charlie Mack W. 4	Holborn
Ted Snow W. 4	Holborn
Ted Beach L. pts. 5	Holborn
(Final of 6st. 12lb. Competition)	
Harry Collins W. ko 5	London
Charlie Mills W. ko 1	London
Bill Wood W. 4	Newmarket
Harry Adams W. ko 1	London
Bill Wood W. 8	Newmarket

1897

Bill Parsons W. 4	Holborn
Con Barrett W. 4	Holborn
Sid Scales L. 5	Holborn
(Final of 7st. 2lb. Competition)	
Harry Tangue W. ko 7	London
Charlie Simpson L. 10	Birmingham
Jack Mitchell W. 4	Birmingham
Harry Ware W. 4	Birmingham
Charlie Simpson W. ko 2	Birmingham
(Final of 8st. 6lb. Competition)	

	Charlie Simpson W. 6	Birmingham
Apr 4	Harry Checketts W. ko 8	Birmingham
	Patsy Walsh W. ko 2	Birmingham
Dec 13	George Corfield W. ko 5	Birmingham
	Bob Ford W. ko 2	Stratford

1898

Oct 27	Mike Sears W. rsf 12	Birmingham
(World 8st. 11lb. Title)		

—	Dick Higgins W. ko 4	Birmingham
	1899	
Feb 23	Bill Newell W. ko 9	Birmingham
May 8	Dave Wallace W. ko 8	Birmingham
Nov 20	Harry Greenfield W. ko 8	London
(English 9st. 2lb. Title)		
	1900	
Apr 12	Will Curley L. 1 (9-11)	Newcastle
	1901	
—	J. Pongo W. ko 4	Dudley
Dec 23	Jemmy Curran D. 20	London
(English Lightweight Title)		
	1902	
Apr 21	Bill Chester W. ko 5	London
(English 9st. 8lb. Title)		
Jun 21	Spike Sullivan W. 15	London
(English 9st. 8lb. Title)		
—	Bill Gray W. ko 2	Barnsley
	1903	
Apr 20	Spike Sullivan W. 15	London
(English Lighweight Title)		
	1905	
May 5	Jimmy Britt L. 20	San Francisco
(World Lightweight Title)		
	1906	
Jan 8	Bob Russell W. 15 (9-10)	Birmingham
(English Lightweight Title)		
Apr 24	Jack Goldswain L. 20	London
(English 10st. Lightweight Title)		
	1909	
Mar 12	Joe Gans nd 10	New York
	1913	
Feb 10	Bill Johnson L. 15	Birmingham

TED WHITE

Born 18th May, 1867.   Charing Cross.

	1887	
Won ABA Heavyweight Title		St. James Hall
	1888	
	Jem Kendrick Lost	Wood Green
	Pat Condon W. 8	Haymarket
	Arthur Bobbett L. 4	Haymarket

	Bill Husband Won	Haymarket

(Pelican Club £15 Compeition)

	Alec Burns Lost	Imperial Theatre

1889

| Feb 23 | Andy Cannon Won | Wood Green |
| — | Jack Richardson Won | Wood Green |

(Final of Frank Hynde's 10st. 4lb. Championship Competition)

Mar 13	Bill Hatcher W. 3	Islington
Mar 14	Ghing Ghook Won	Islington
Mar 16	Sam Baxter L. 4	Islington

(Final of Charlie White's 10st. 4lb. Championship Competition)

Apr 23	Jem Burchell W. 3	Wood Green
Apr 25	Jack Jones W. f. 2	Wood Green
Apr 25	Bat Mullins W. 4	Wood Green

(Final of Frank Hynde's 11st. Championship Competition)

—	George Burgin W. 6	Wood Green
—	Arthur Bobbett W. ko 9	Waite's School of Arms
Oct 25	Tom Meadows W. f. 7	Kennington

1890

| — | Alec Burns W. 7 | Haymarket |
| Jun — | Ted Rich W. ko 2 | Haymarket |

1891

| Mar 7 | John O'Brien L. ko 9 | Haymarket |
| Jun 10 | Jack Welland W. 12 | N.S.C. |

1892

| Feb 8 | Billy McCarthy L. 13 | N.S.C. |

1893

Mar 6	Harry Holdsworth W. 3	N.S.C.
Mar 6	George Chrisp W. 3	N.S.C.
Mar 6	Alf Bowman W. 4	N.S.C.

(Final of Middleweight Championship Competition)

| Apr 24 | George Chrisp W. 20 (154lb.) | N.S.C. |

(English Middleweight Title)

1894

| Jan 15 | Anthony Diamond W. 20 | N.S.C. |

(English Middleweight Title)

1895

| Nov 25 | Kid McCoy W. 10 (152lb.) | N.S.C. |

1896

| Feb 3 | Tom Tracey Exh. 3 | N.S.C. |
| Jun 1 | Dido Plumb W. rsf 16 | N.S.C. |

(English Middleweight Title) (158lb.)

JIM WILLIAMS

Born 1st May, 1876.   Marylebone, London

	Undated Contests	
	Tom Sexton W. 2	Leeds
	Jim Carlin W. 2	Leeds
	Dave Baws W. 2	
	Dick Player W. 2	
	Tom Smith W. 1	
	George Fowler W. 1	Holborn
	Ginger Price W. 1	Holborn
	Harry Ware W. 2	Holborn
(Final of 7st. 4lb. Competition)		
	Johnny Thomas Won	Sheffield
	Young Moran W. 12	
	Jim Collins W. 7	
	Johnny Thomas W. 9	
	Harry Ware Drew	
	Jack Maloney W. 4	
	Bill Davis W. 2	
	Tom Wheeler W. 4	
	T. Hughes W. 2	
	Tom O'Grady W. 4	
	Tom Pearson Won	
	Bandy Chambers Won	
	1893	
Mar 3	Terry O'Neil W. 2	London
	1894	
Jan 15	Jumbo Patch W. 6	Kilburn
—	George Murray Won	Leeds
(Final of 7st. Championship Competition)		
	1895	
Feb 6	Jack Maloney W. 4	—
Feb 12	Albert Gould L. f. 1	Kilburn
(English 7st. 6lb. Title)		
Mar —	Goody Jacobs Won	Holborn
Mar —	Alf Carey Won	Holborn
Mar —	Dick Parkes Won	Holborn
(Final of 7st. 8lb. Championship Competition)		
Dec 20	Ernie Stanton L. ko 3	N.S.C.

1896

| Mar 23 | Tom Turner W. 20 | N.S.C. |
| Apr 13 | Wag Ward W. ko 4 | N.S.C. |

1897

| — | Sailor Richardson W. 7 | N.S.C. |

1898

Feb —	Dick Parkes L. pts.	London
Mar 1	Harry Saphir W. 2	Sheffield
Apr 18	Harry Ware L. rsf 9	N.S.C.
Sep 5	George Corfield W. 12	Sheffield
Nov 21	Dick Johnson W. ko 12	Gateshead
—	Ted Beach Won	—

(Final of 6st. 10lb. Championship Competition)

1900

Mar 30	Dave Morbin Won	Wonderland
Mar 30	Ted Goodson Won	Wonderland
Apr 6	Patsy Walsh L. 6	Wonderland

(Final of 8st. 6lb. Championship Competition)

1902

| Jan 27 | Pedler Palmer W. ko 2 | N.S.C. |

(English Bantamweight Title) (8st. 4lb.)

| May 12 | Andrew Tokell L. f. 10 | N.S.C. |

(English 8st. 2lb. Title)

| Oct 23 | Pedler Palmer L. 15 | London |

1903

| Jul 11 | Digger Stanley L. 6 | London |

TOM WOODLEY

Fulham, London.

Undated Contests
J. Wells Won
J. Wells Won
Harry Dove Won
Harry Dove Won
Dick Chandler Won
Archie Phillips Won
Driver Pinchin Won
Jem Styles Won
Ginger Osborne Won
Arthur Lock L. 3
(Final of Open 9st. 8lb. Competition)

| Harry Neumier Won | Wonderland |

	Jewey Cooke L. 6	—
	1896	
Nov 8	Alf Duff W. ko 5	London
	1898	
Jan 17	Jerry Driscoll L. 20	N.S.C.
Feb 18	Driver Welsh W. ret. 2	N.S.C.
	1899	
Feb —	Jerry Driscoll L. 10	Ramsgate
—	Pat Daley L. 15	N.S.C.
	1900	
Apr 26	George Penny W. 10	Wonderland
May 21	George Penny W. 10	N.S.C.
	1902	
Jan 20	Jem Styles W. ko 14	Newcastle-upon-Tyne
	(English 10st. 6lb. Title)	
Sep 15	Eddie Connolly W. pts. 11	New Adelphi Club
	(English 10st. 6lb. Title)	
	1903	
Jan 26	Eddie Connolly L. 15	N.S.C.
	(English 10st. 6lb. Title)	
Apr 25	Charlie Knock L. ko 4	London
	1905	
Feb 20	Charlie Knock W. f. 5	Wonderland
	(English 10st. 4lb. Title)	

TOM ALLEN
English Heavyweight Champion
1877-1882

L

BILL BAXTER
English Bantamweight Champion
1888-1890

SAMUEL BLAKELOCK
Winner of 9st. Championship Competition
1886

CHARLEY DAVIS
English Middleweight Champion
1873-1876

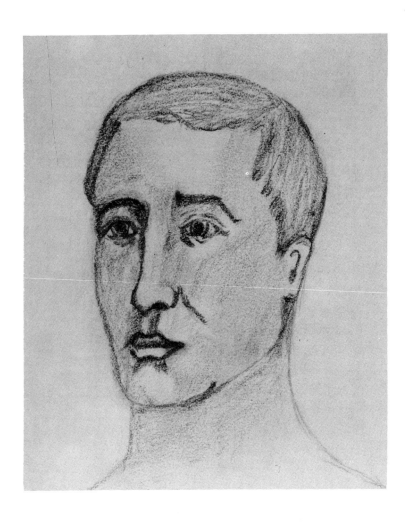

GEORGE DOVE
English Bantamweight Champion
1872-1877

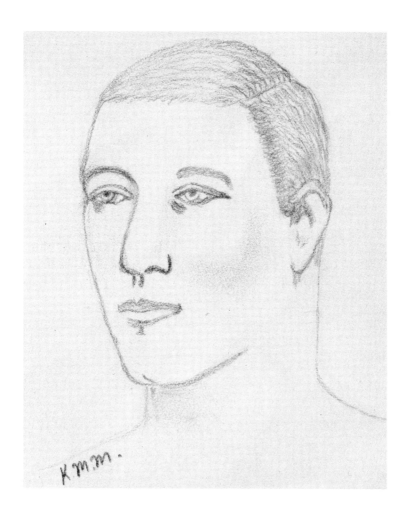

DENNY HARRINGTON
World Middleweight Champion
1878-1880

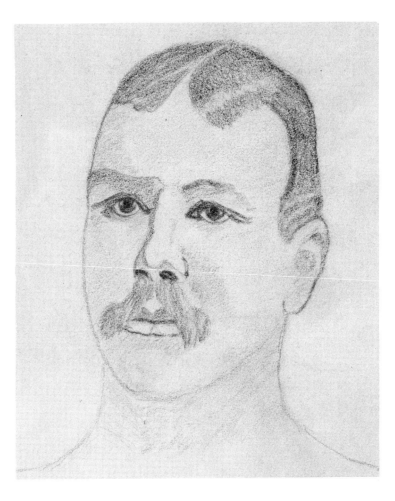

JOHN KNIFTON
English Heavyweight Champion
The First Heavyweight Champion under Marquis of Queensbury Rules
1877

TOMMY ORANGE
English Featherweight Champion
1880

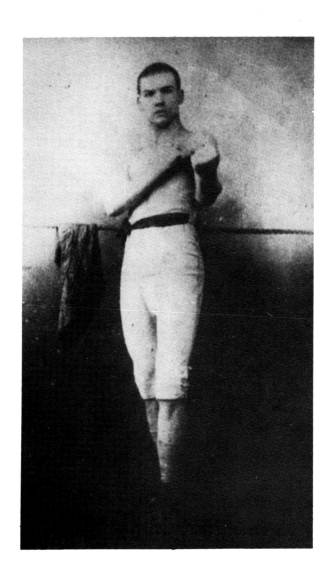

TED PRITCHARD
English Heavyweight and
Middleweight Champion in the 1890s

WILLIAM SHERIFF
World Middleweight Champion
1880-1883

TED WHITE
English Middleweight Champion
1893-1896

TOM CAUSER
English Lightweight Champion
1894-1898

GEORGE CORFIELD
English 8st. Champion
1895-1896

XIII

P.O. MATTHEW CURRAN
British Heavyweight Champion
1910-1912

XIV

ANTHONY DIAMOND
English Middleweight Champion
1898

HARRY GREENFIELD
English Featherweight Champion
1897-1899

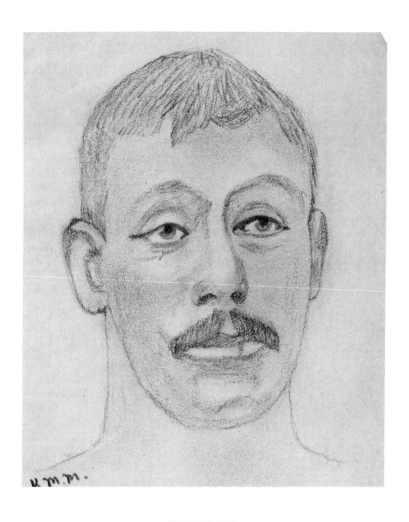

FRED JOHNSON
English Featherweight Champion
1888-1893

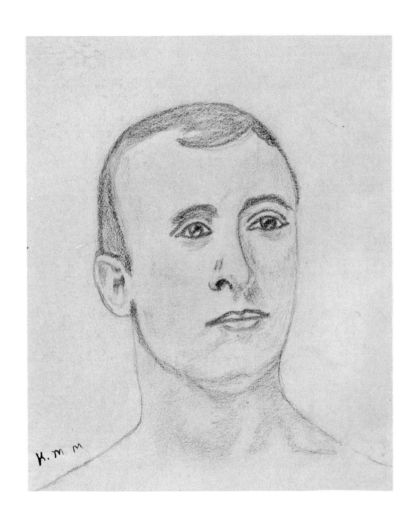

CHAPPIE MORAN
English 7st. 7lb. Champion
1894

HARRY OVERTON
English 9st. Champion
1890-1891

JACK SCALES
Winner of Heavyweight Championship Belt
1902

HARRY SPURDEN
English 9st. Champion
1890-1895

TOM TURNER
Winner of 8st. 8lb. Championship Competition
1898

CHARLIE WILSON
English Heavyweight Claimant
1902

XXIII

TOM WOODLEY
English 10st. 6lb. Champion
1902